What Was I Thinking?

Adventures of a Woman Sailing Solo

PAMELA ROY BENDALL

Cataloguing in Publication Information
Available from Library and Archives Canada
ISBN 978-0-9921413-0-1

Cover photo: *Precious Metal* crossing the bar at Bahia del Sol, El Salvador. Taken by Bill Yeargan. Bill and his wife Jean Strain are the organizers of the Annual El Salvador Cruiser's Rally. Author photo: Gaylean Sutcliffe

Cover and interior design by Vivalogue Publishing
www.vivalogue.com

Printed and bound in Canada

Published by
Pamela Bendall Enterprises
www.pamelabendall.com

What Was I Thinking? is dedicated to my two precious grandchildren, Maddy and George, and to all of my future grandchildren and future generations who haven't arrived in this world. Sadly, I am and likely will always be, a long-distance Grandma. This book provides Maddy and George with a greater insight about their loving Gramela who lives far, far away on a boat and can only visit their home in London, England, on occasion – which is never enough.

Author's Note

I have taken the liberty of changing the names of characters in certain situations – particularly in a limited number of sections that could be deemed derogatory to the local people involved. Secondly, while this book is autobiographical in nature, my interpretations of certain situations may be different from other peoples' perceptions of how various events unfolded. I apologize if I have unintentionally misrepresented anyone's character or version of any incident in the story.

Table of Contents

Acknowledgements

How do I begin to thank the great number of people who have made this story possible? The list is almost as long as the book itself!

My long-time friend Joanne Vickery took on the greatest number of roles in this voyage and therefore deserves the greatest amount of credit. Joanne dutifully handled all of my administration in Canada, stored my 'stuff', provided a base to call home, answered my calls of anguish from distant corners of the world, propped me up when I was down and visited me on numerous occasions in some highly obscure locations. Joanne – I feel honoured and so thankful to have you as my friend!

A great number of people devoted their holidays to share in this experience and help me with certain legs of the voyage during my first few years. Ilver Villani deserves notable credit for his support and participation during the first two years. I am extremely grateful to all other visitors (and you know who you are) who made the effort to join me and provided their continued support, enthusiasm and expertise. Finally, Henry Robinson, aboard his catamaran *Rapscullion*, who was my buddy, companion and saviour in a number of situations. In my mind, he is a saint. Without Henry's constant vigilance and ability to repair certain problems aboard my boat, I question whether this book would have such a happy ending.

My family provided terrific support. Both sons Sam and Charlie were often at the end of the phone line and sent emails providing me with the necessary encouragement and wisdom to "stick it out." Their wives (my daughters-in-law), Lizz and Catherine, also played invaluable roles in keeping my spirits high. My sister

Pat and her husband Peter have been incredibly supportive in so many ways. They have been my cheerleaders, promoters, friends and supporters throughout the entire voyage and throughout my life. They are the very best sister and brother-in-law anyone could ever have! I simply can't thank them enough.

I am also grateful to my late parents Gordon and Margaret, who instilled the necessary confidence and abilities in my childhood that have allowed my goals and dreams in life to be fulfilled. My sisters Jennifer and Nancy, as well as nieces, nephews and extended family also played supportive roles in this voyage.

A very special mention goes to Ron Duquette for his support, enthusiasm and guidance. Ron also devoted a tremendous amount of time and professionalism towards producing the promotional video for this book and my upcoming professional speaking endeavours. My behind-the-scenes editor and friend, who chooses to remain anonymous, was invaluable in providing me with constructive commentaries and continued encouragement throughout my entire writing process.

I could never have completed this voyage without the noteworthy assistance of so many competent and devoted fellow cruisers who faithfully came to my rescue and assisted during *Precious Metal's* challenging situations: Paul on *Sunrunner*, John on *Millennium*, John and John aboard *Outta Here* and *Sea Quest* and so many additional capable people were always willing and able to teach and assist as necessary in my times of trouble.

Finally, I could never have accomplished this dream without my wonderful friends. Friends in Canada, cruising friends, squash friends, girlfriends, local friends that I made in each country and everyone who wrote letters of interest and encouragement during this voyage. I'm so fortunate to have so many terrific friends in my life.

I am forever grateful to everyone involved.

Captain Pamelita!

As I was referred to throughout Peru and Central America

Preface

What was I thinking when I decided to embrace my epiphany and devote my life to sailing and *Precious Metal*? At the time, I was driving around in a sexy sports car, wearing designer clothes, owned a fabulous home on the ocean and had manicured nails. I was enjoying the best wines, restaurants, single malt scotch and essentially living an opulent high-end stock broker lifestyle. My only venture into a hardware store would have been to buy fitness equipment or perhaps a light bulb.

Since that time I've sailed over 25,000 ocean miles from as far north as Alaska to Central and South America and a multitude of places in between – mostly single-handedly. I've spent a lot of my time in impoverished Third World countries. *Precious Metal*, Riley and I have endured virtually every ocean challenge imaginable including major storms, loss of steering and being hit by lightning at sea 200 miles from our destination. My eyes and mind have opened. This has been far more than a voyage; rather, it's been an incredible journey and one that I could never have dreamed.

Seven years later, I no longer own a car. But that's not quite correct. Actually, my car is a nine-foot dinghy with an eight horsepower Yamaha outboard engine. My possessions fill a small corner of a friend's basement in Canada, although I own a house in Canada that is rented. My wardrobe consists of brightly coloured short skirts, tank tops, bathing suits and designer flip flops. My nails are short due to continual boat maintenance and my hair is bleached blond due to exposure to the sun. I can diagnose and fix almost everything on my boat. None of my friends in Canada would believe how low my wine standards have fallen – the only available wine in Central America is from a box called 'Clos' - which we jokingly refer to as 'clos to wine'. That said, I still enjoy a wonderful meal, as well as a decadent wine and scotch when they're available!

I essentially live a self-sufficient lifestyle. I make my own water and power, rely on solar panels and leave a very small carbon footprint on the planet. Other than the never-ending maintenance and repairs of my boat, my life is simple. I have now, finally, discovered the art of living my dream.

As you'll discover, many 'What was I thinking?' moments took place to reach this stage of contentment. It took time to evolve and discover what I was really looking for in life. Looking back on my life in Canada, I was on a machine – filling every minute of every day with activity. The sailing dream that I initially embraced seven years ago and the way that it has unfolded are worlds apart. We can dream and we can make plans according to how we see the world at the time, but until we actually enact that dream, we will never know where it will lead.

During this voyage, I've experienced highs that adjectives simply can't describe. I've also endured lows when I had to dig very deep and it took every ounce of fortitude and wherewithal to survive. I've missed my family and friends enormously. I've been extremely lonely at times. I've been frustrated by the enormous task of running and maintaining the boat and at times I've been afraid, even terrified. I've spent a lot of time alone; the longest period was two weeks when the only communication was periodic VHF radio calls. The transition of going from an intensely active lifestyle to one of solitude and self-preservation has been enormous. While the challenges of this voyage were incredibly difficult at times, I would never have given up the experience for anything in the world.

The first six chapters of this book (Section One) leading up to my 2008 offshore departure from Canada, set the stage for my amazing voyage insofar as I needed the experience of operating my boat before I could venture further. These first chapters are by no means insignificant; however, I believe that my learning curve truly began when I left Canada in 2008. As you read through each chapter my hope is that you'll be entertained by my experiences and digest the messages and lessons learned – both implied and overtly stated. More importantly, my sincere desire is that you'll be inspired to follow your passions and dreams. If I can do it, anyone can.

Section One

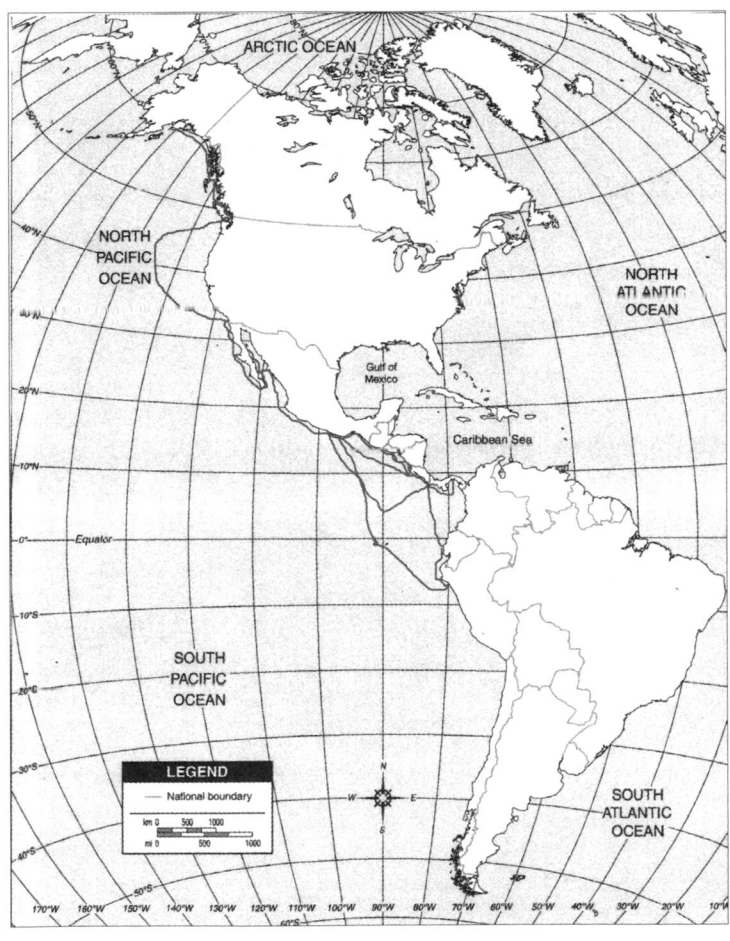

Precious Metal's *route from Alaska to Mexico, Galapagos Islands, Peru, Ecuador, Cocos Islands, Central America and Panama*

CHAPTER 1

Introducing the Main Characters

My Precious Boat

Precious Metal could be re-named 'Wish-list' because when I sailed the South Pacific in the late 1980s with my former husband (Michael) and two young children (Sam and Charlie – ages 4 and 10), I had a list in the back of my log book highlighting important features I dreamed of having on my future offshore sailboat. *Precious Metal* was custom built by Kristen Yachts in Sidney, British Columbia, and features most of these desirable amenities.

Steel construction was foremost in my mind for safety reasons. Forty-six feet seemed to be the optimum length; small enough to handle alone, yet large enough for comfortable living space and extensive storage. I wanted this boat to feel like a home and not as though I was camping on the ocean.

Her luxurious hand-crafted custom cherry wood interior and traditional teak and holly flooring throughout the boat is a testimony to the builder's labour of love. The envious dream of all offshore captains is *Precious Metal*'s walk-in, full head-room, engine room. Amongst the many shop tools on the eight-foot work bench is the *pièce de résistance* drill press. With a fuel capacity of 500 gallons and 300 gallon water tanks (as well as a fresh water-maker), the 100-horsepower Isuzu engine has a 2500-mile range.

Ahead of her time, a unique design feature of *Precious Metal* is her raised salon allowing a 270-degree view of the ocean while being comfortably seated in the centre stage salon, alongside a full-size chart storage table. The spacious master suite boasts every yachting woman's fantasy – a deluxe full size bathtub. This up-scale aft suite also includes a queen-size bed, voluminous cabinet space and a separate head, shower and powder room.

Precious Metal is a cutter rig with Leisure Furl in-boom furling and an electric winch – which I kiss every morning when I have my morning coffee. I installed the new main sail, roller furling and electric winch prior to my departure from Canada, which has made a tremendous improvement in the ease with which I raise and lower my sails. The state-of-the-art davit system, aft swim deck with shower and swim ladder are essentials in tropical waters. The full-size cockpit converts into a double bed and has surrounding curtains for all weather conditions. She was built to sail anywhere in the world in style, extreme comfort and absolute safety.

While this was my dream boat, my former husband Brian Haley also played a role in the decision-making process of

Precious Metal's *precious exterior*

Precious Metal's *interior main salon*

construction, sails and rigging, as well as the interior layout. Victoria's Greg Marshall was the naval architect and Reg Whitman was the boat builder. After we purchased the hull in December 1998, it took another six months of construction and due diligence before *Precious Metal* was lowered into the water for her grand Champagne Christening in July 1999.

My Precious Dog Riley

It's difficult to imagine a more wonderful companion for this voyage than Riley. This Cavalier King Charles Spaniel is clearly the most exceptional of all the dogs that I've owned in my life. Born in 2000 in Sooke, British Columbia (breeder Angela Thomas), both of his parents were champion dogs. His cuddly, comforting, adaptable and extremely friendly nature has captured the hearts of everyone he has encountered throughout the entire voyage. I'm seriously considering my next book to be entitled, *What Was Riley Thinking?*

Riley has been sailing since he was a puppy and has always been agile enough to climb the companionway stairs, jump on the couches and wander to the bow to do his business without

Riley proudly wearing his designer life jacket

hesitation. He sleeps for long hours when we're at sea and loves his beach walks when we're at anchor. His favourite pastime is chasing crabs and snails on the beach along with endless hours of cuddles, lots of treats and attention. I tell people that he's my guard dog; however, he would be the first to welcome a pirate or bandit aboard with his huge brown eyes and wagging tail.*

My Introduction to Sailing

My love for sailing and living on the ocean began in the early 1980s when I lived in the Yukon with my former husband Michael and our two young children Sam and Charlie. After taking all of the recommended Canadian Yachting Association courses and spending our holidays on sailing excursions in tropical regions, in 1980 we finally purchased our first sailboat *Kluane*, which was a Beneteau First 38. Michael had always dreamed of sailing offshore and in 1986 our family moved to

Sadly, since the first edition of this book, my precious Riley has gone to Doggie Heaven. He was my most wonderful companion, soulmate, pride and sailor. He was loved by all who met him from around the world. He is truly missed, and will always be in my thoughts and prayers.

Victoria, British Columbia, where we prepared *Kluane* for her ocean adventure to the South Pacific.

My first book, entitled *Kids for Sail* (Orca Book Publishers, 1991), is the story of our voyage from Victoria to New Zealand between May 1986 to August 1988. Sam and Charlie (aged 10 and 4 at the time of our departure) were home-schooled throughout our 35,000-mile voyage. Our initial route took us from Victoria, Canada, to Hawaii, Fanning and Palmyra Islands, Tonga, Fiji and New Zealand – where Michael obtained a six-month medical opportunity in Greymouth on the South Island and both children were enrolled in school. It was during this time that I wrote the manuscript *Kids for Sail*.

We became more adventurous during our second year and sailed from New Zealand back to Fiji, followed by the Solomon Islands, Papua New Guinea, Micronesia, Guam and finally Japan. During our most incredible 10 months in Japan we sailed from the southernmost corner of Amami Oshima through the Inland Sea to Nagasaki, Fukuoka, Hiroshima and eventually left *Kluane* in the hands of a paid skipper and two crew in Osaka. Our hired crew intended to sail *Kluane* across the North Pacific waters to Alaska where we planned to re-join the boat in early August and sail down the coast to our new home in Vancouver. Unfortunately, these plans didn't quite unfold as we hoped.*

Admittedly, *Kids for Sail* is now somewhat dated, but it does provide for an interesting read insofar as the advances in technology for boats has been enormous in these past three decades. Most of our navigation across the oceans in the 1980s was done by sextant, using lengthy mathematical calculations just to find our position. I still remember a fellow sailor showing me a small calculator that he had bought in New Zealand that calculated the latitude and longitude from sun and moon sights and I was completely overwhelmed. We finally splurged in Fiji and bought our first single sideband/ham radio for communication. Until that time we were completely alone at sea. We never owned a radar. Our letters to family and friends

See Appendix I for details of this story.

were hand-written or typed on an old-fashioned typewriter and mailed overseas which seemed to take forever. In fact, the entire manuscript of *Kids for Sail* was produced on one of the first fancy electric typewriters that corrected mistakes without having to use liquid white-out!

Sam is now 36 and Charlie recently turned 30. I'm somewhat biased and incredibly proud in saying that both of my boys have developed into interesting, healthy, successful and somewhat worldly men. Sam continued to sail long after our voyage and by the time he reached 30 he had only lived 10 years of his life on land. He is now settled in London, England, with his wonderful wife Lizz and my two young grandchildren, Maddy and George. Sam's sailing adventures took him over 200,000 ocean miles and he sailed around both the Cape of Good Hope and Cape Horn twice. Charlie developed into more of a land-based, social individual with tremendous character and initiative. He was a star basketball player in his youth, enjoys a serious game of squash and recently earned his degree in business. Charlie currently resides in Newfoundland, Canada, with his lovely wife Catherine.

As you'll read in Appendix I, extenuating circumstances caused *Kluane* to be sold in Japan in 1989. I subsequently owned five sailboats prior to custom building *Precious Metal* in 1999. Needless to say, my passion for sailing and exploring the oceans has been enormous since our family's cruising voyage in the South Pacific. In addition to cruising the entire British Columbia coastline over the past 30 years, I raced as the navigator in the Victoria to Maui (1992) and Marblehead (1996) offshore races, and volunteered as media and public relations chairperson and Royal Vancouver Yacht Club chairperson for the Victoria–Maui race between the years of 2002 to 2008.

My Epiphany

Life curiously presents us with monumental, life-changing curve balls when we least expect them. Surprisingly, I retrace my epic epiphany back to soot – grimy, filthy, black soot.

Yes, my incredible five-year, 25,000-mile ocean voyage began because of some wayward boat exhaust on an early October day during my 50th year, which was, until my epiphany, the darkest year of my life.

Turning 50 was a tumultuous time for me. My two wonderful sons had recently left the nest and my powerful maternal instincts were painfully missing my boys. I was going through a divorce which seemed to tear apart many of my solid roots and future dreams. My investment business had been sold three years prior to my divorce and I had no career in sight. During my separation, I immersed myself in completing my Masters Degree in Communication at Royal Roads University near Victoria, British Columbia, and simply buried my head in the required research to complete my schooling and thesis.*

Exhausted from a cross-Canada flight, only one of three messages on my answering machine mattered – the one about my boat. My mind was deflated after an abominably disastrous road trip across the country pitching a new business endeavour that I sensed would not succeed. I simply wanted to escape by going to bed and forgetting the events of the past week.

Listening to the phone message, one more worry was added to my list of burdens woes. The marina attendant who was in charge of my sailboat informed me that, "*Precious Metal* is covered in soot and should be cleaned immediately." He explained that a fishing boat with a compromised exhaust system was moored beside me and spewed oily soot throughout the entire night all over my spotless white decks. "Wonderful. That's all I need to top off the week," I grumbled to myself, as I crawled into bed alone, totally disillusioned with life, feeling pathetically sorry for myself.

My 13 years as a Canadian West Coast stock broker had embedded a permanent early morning alarm system into my

---

* Mergers and Acquisitions *was a fascinating study and in theory it would set the stage for my exciting career as a communications consultant in the board rooms of M&A activity across the nation. My hot-off-the-press research for my thesis led to the establishment of a new consulting business call Merge Communications, which, after the aforementioned road trip, never got off the ground.*

brain. Rarely do I sleep past 6.00am, regardless of significant time changes. Furthermore, mornings are always an exciting time for me and I usually jump out of bed with gusto, ready to take on the day ahead. True to form I bounced out of bed early the following morning, donning my grubbiest attire to ready myself for the task of cleaning soot. I hastily drove to my girlfriend Joanne's house to pick up my little dog Riley, shared some conversation over a quick cup of coffee to catch up on our past week and then darted to the marina before the dreaded car traffic could build.

The soot problem was far worse than I had imagined. My poor boat was laden with a quarter-inch of grimy, black exhaust from bow to stern, covering virtually every exposed area. Reluctantly, I set the stage for the day ahead: put on my favourite tunes in high volume, brought out the cleaning supplies, packed some beer in the fridge and donned my knee pads – knowing it was going to be a very long and physically demanding day.

In short order, my scrubbing adopted a musical rhythm to the beat of my favourite music. The warm sun magically brightened the sky. People walking the docks stopped by for brief friendly chats and I savoured the occasional refreshing beer to quench my parched throat. The day was unfolding much better than I had anticipated. Surprisingly, I felt quite content.

Yet, I could not help but think about the disastrous events of the previous week and the disappointing business meetings. I simply couldn't shake off my disillusionment. My former colleagues seemed totally uninterested in my hot-off-the-press, innovative and enlightened business model designed to foster better communication in the merger and acquisition of companies.

Also, there was a gnawing undercurrent and deep personal reservation about returning to the corporate world. Everyone I had met seemed to be so stressed, pre-occupied and exhausted. I suddenly realized that I was once one of them, maybe worse! They all politely gave me the time to pitch my business plan; then changed the subject completely by eagerly asking questions like, "So how's the sailing?" Were they subconsciously trying to tell me something? The very reason for my early retirement from the investment business was blatantly manifesting itself before my eyes. Do I really want to go back?

What was I thinking, expecting instant enthusiasm for a mergers and acquisitions (M&A) communications consulting business in an industry that's male-dominated, traditional in nature and indifferent to unquantifiable strategies that aren't 'bottom line' oriented? Communications are too 'fluffy' to take seriously in the intense, hard-core board rooms of M&A activity. I realized that my business was going to be a tough sell, needing lots of blood, sweat and tears – mostly tears.

As my scrubbing progressed at a snail's pace, I realized that in spite of the rigorous task at hand, I would rather be cleaning soot on my boat than return to the corporate environment.

Suddenly a light began to shine and it wasn't only the sun…

My mind raced into high gear. I owned a fabulous boat that was specifically built for offshore sailing. I was an accomplished sailor. I had always dreamed of returning to the cruising world. I probably had enough money and assets to survive frugally. I was single. My kids had left the nest. I answered to no one.

At that moment, my epiphany manifested itself: *"I'm free to make any decision I want in life. Rarely in life do we have opportunities to change course and follow our passions. If sailing and* Precious Metal *are my passion, I'm going to follow my heart and make them the focus of my life from this day forward."*

I scrubbed and scrubbed in a wild frenzy wondering how I could incorporate *Precious Metal* into a viable business opportunity. The concept of operating a charter business came to the forefront. After all, I had been exploring the entire British Columbia coastline for 25 years and I would love nothing better than to show off this absolutely stunning region to visitors from around the world. Additionally, I enjoyed engaging with people – socializing, cooking and playing hostess. What a perfect match for me and my precious *Precious Metal*. She would finally earn her keep!

It didn't take long before thoughts of my company Merge Communications disappeared, replaced by visions of a vital new charter business. The adrenalin rush was overwhelming. I wanted to do a jig on the bow of my boat! At last, I was able to climb out of the deep dark hole that had absorbed me for eight months since my marriage separation.

The name 'Precious Yacht Charters' stuck. It wouldn't let go. It had a wonderful ring. The hasty decision was made: I was now the new owner and operator of Precious Yacht Charters. I was in fast-forward motion and never looked back. An exciting new chapter was unfolding and I was exuberant.

Ironically, I wished I could find that old, toothless fisherman – the owner of the decrepit rusty crab boat that spewed soot – to express my gratitude for the epiphany he initiated. If he only knew the incredible impact his filthy soot had on my life and the amazing adventures I was about to embark on.

Turning 50 wasn't so bad after all – in fact, it was becoming wonderfully exciting!

CHAPTER 2

Circumnavigating Vancouver Island

June 2005

C IRCUMNAVIGATING VANCOUVER ISLAND had always been a dream of mine and an excellent way to gain my confidence in operating *Precious Metal* on my own. My girlfriend Jane Harper, who owned a 50-foot sailboat named *Ten* also had this desire and during a casual lunch at the Royal Vancouver Yacht Club we convinced ourselves that "two blondes on two beautiful boats" circumnavigating Vancouver Island would be a terrific adventure. Before we knew it we toasted our glasses towards committing our summer to this major undertaking. This proved to be the first of many 'What was I thinking?' moments.

Organizing our eight-week voyage was a logistical nightmare. We decided to invite our friends to join each of our boats for week-long stints throughout the circumnavigation. Regular transportation routes on the east side of the Island easily facilitated locations where people could embark and disembark our vessels; however, on the virtually uninhabited west coast, it wasn't that simple. We had to hire local float planes to transport people and supplies to and from the boats each week. Fortunately the entire process went like clockwork. In fact, it was a terrific summer, albeit with a few terrifying, character-building moments.

As our late-June departure date approached, I began to feel incredibly apprehensive about our upcoming voyage. So many wonderful friends had committed their summer holiday aboard *Precious Metal*; otherwise, I'm confident that I would have aborted the voyage. In addition to my apprehension towards handling the boat, my heart was still aching over my separation and I knew that I would be revisiting so many places that would painfully ignite fond memories of my buried past. Ultimately, I acquiesced to honouring my commitment to my friends and I reluctantly forced myself to keep moving forward with our circumnavigation itinerary.

Suddenly departure week was upon us. My first week-long guest was incredibly enthusiastic. Angelo was an avid athlete in his late 30s who was keen to learn sailing and share in my new adventure aboard *Precious Metal*. In fact, Angelo phoned early in our departure week asking how he could help or contribute towards the voyage. "Wonderful," I replied. "We'll need fresh spices on the west coast. Please arrange a portable flower basket full of your favourite spices." There was a long pause before Angelo responded. "I've never been much of a gardener but I'll happily try."

What was I thinking? In hindsight, a strong capable male was offering to help me prepare *Precious Metal* and I asked him to bring spices? Clearly I didn't know what I didn't know – because if I did know what I didn't know he would have been changing filters, tightening hose clamps, greasing and lubricating, changing oil – and there would be no end to his list of possible chores. That said, Angelo dutifully arrived with his planter of spices and I was naively absolutely thrilled with his generous contribution to our voyage.

The first three weeks of the northbound journey were fairly uneventful. I hosted a number of guests during the subsequent weeks who were all fun, engaging and helpful. My squash buddies from Vancouver, Bob Waldron and Dave Geekie, came aboard during the second week and another friend, George Galbraith, joined *Precious Metal* for the third week. We explored fabulous cruising grounds and stopped each evening along the magnificent British Columbia coastline. Jane's departure from Vancouver was delayed so we decided to meet in the small community of Port

Hardy at the northern tip of the Island where I had scheduled six days for re-provisioning and possible repairs.

Ironically, those six nights in Port Hardy set the stage for a seven-year relationship with the local marina owner named Ilver. The six glorious days were comprised of many magical moments when the sun shone continuously (you don't want to be anywhere else on a sunny day), the marina life and community felt uniquely engaging and a hint of romance with Ilver heightened my female instincts for the first time in ages. As I untied *Precious Metal's* docking lines in Port Hardy bound for the intrepid west coast, my heart sensed a throbbing tug and a longing to return to Port Hardy at some future date.

Cape Scott is located on the north-western tip of Vancouver Island and has a treacherous reputation amongst boaters. The relatively shallow bank that stretches out over 20 miles from the shoreline is also the site of the confluence of several major ocean currents. In addition, the weather can be challenging on the west coast. These factors can contribute to horrendous sailing conditions characterised by huge vertical swells and exceptionally strong winds for most of each day – if you're lucky.

Angelo had re-joined *Precious Metal* for his second stint, along with a mechanically inclined friend named Greg. As the waves continued to build around Cape Scott, so did Angelo's seasickness. In a desperate measure, we dressed him in a full wet weather suit and tied him to the lifelines so he could safely manage his vomiting overboard. There was no turning back or respite from the nasty sea conditions until we arrived at our next stop at Winter Harbour – approximately six long hours away. Poor Angelo. I felt so incredibly helpless and sorry for my new sailing companion.

Maybe Monday...

The rain poured continuously for the following two weeks. Everything aboard was soaking wet and our spirits were dwindling. Bobby Waldron, Angelo and a wonderful female friend Jan Canning (whom I had worked with in the investment business) participated in this leg of the west coast voyage around the Brooks Peninsula. Jan was an experienced sailor and competent racer. One gloomy Thursday afternoon when we were tied to a fuel dock in Kyuquot Sound, a wise-looking elderly First Nations chief sauntered by *Precious Metal*.

"Does it always rain this hard?" I asked. "Yup," he replied. "Will we ever see sunshine between now and the end of the summer?" I asked hopefully. "Nope," he retorted as he wandered away from us. Suddenly he turned and said, "Maybe Monday." We all cheered in unison and for the following three days and nights we made up slogans and sang jingles about 'Monday' – forever hopeful that our wise old chief knew his weather.

Monday arrived without a cloud in the sky! Our chief's miraculous weather forecast was amazing. With lifted spirits we headed to a highly recommended beach at Rugged Point Marine Park which, according to our charts, was just around the corner from our anchorage. After securing our dinghies on shore we followed a windy path through the forest and suddenly stood in awe as we stepped into the clearing. This incredibly spectacular, endless stretch of white sand and rocky outcrops was absolutely breath-taking, representing the very best of Mother Nature.

Throughout the entire day we all frolicked about like young children at the world's largest playground. The weather was uncharacteristically hot allowing us to body surf for hours in the strong shoreline swells. We even took turns taking Riley body surfing in the waves. Our private beach extended for miles and miles and our guests from both boats played the entire day away. It was one of those glorious days in life that few people ever have the good fortune to experience.

All good things eventually come to an end and at 5.00pm we sadly forced ourselves to abandon our wonderful surroundings and find a suitable anchorage for the night.

The elation from our jovial day quickly took a horrible turn as we entered a small uncharted channel towards our next anchorage that had been recommended by a local fisherman just inside Esmeralda Inlet. What was I thinking? I had taken advice from an unknown source without adequate charts in an extremely remote area. Eight-tenths of a mile from the head of the channel lay an uncharted sand bar and *Precious Metal's* 50,000 pounds instantly grounded into the soft bottom.

My heart pounded frantically as I tried every boat manoeuvre to release her from the ocean floor. There was nothing we could do to rectify the situation and at 7.00pm we finally came to terms with our disastrous situation – *Precious Metal* would be grounded for the night in the middle of absolutely nowhere, with no apparent recourse other than to wait for the next high tide.

Ten had been following behind *Precious Metal* and was able to remain outside the bay to avoid the innocuous sand bar. After lengthy discussion we decided to shuttle two of Jane's most capable male crew (Greg – who had previously sailed around Cape Scott with me – and Ron Barr who was a competent sailor) to *Precious Metal* for the night, in exchange for my crew. Anchored reasonably close by, Jane did a masterful job of providing support as needed for *Precious Metal* – including a wonderful midnight feast of tasty sandwiches.

According to the tide tables, the tide would continue to fall until 10.00pm and then it would gradually rise until 2.00am. The subsequent morning low tide was extremely low; therefore, if *Precious Metal* was not able to float during the 2.00am high tide, she would likely become shipwrecked in Esmeralda Sound and possibly never float again. I was both extremely sad and worried about the ultimate fate of my precious yacht.

As predicted, the tide continued to descend until *Precious Metal* was resting at 45 degrees on her side. The night was pitch black without a star in the sky and somewhat overcast with periods of wind and rain. Greg, Ron and I tightly sealed the entire through-hull openings on the boat and continuously circled *Precious Metal* checking for possible water leaks. Occasionally, I would venture inside the boat, which was like walking through a haunted house in the dark. Otherwise, we patiently sat on the high deck telling stories and stalling for time as the tide performed its duty.

At exactly 10.00pm we dangled our plumb line over the side

of the boat and recorded our lowest water reading before the tide began to flood and gradually bring *Precious Metal* upright. This brought relief knowing that our tidal readings for that location were accurate. By midnight we were becoming extremely anxious knowing that the circumstances taking place over the next two hours would determine *Precious Metal's* fate. Watching paint dry would be more stimulating then waiting for the tide to move. A strong weather system began to build, reinforcing my concern that I not only had to release *Precious Metal* from the sand bar, but as well, I needed to drive her to safety in deteriorating weather conditions in absolute darkness.

As 2.00am approached our conversations dissipated in exchange for quiet contemplation. My route out of the bay towards *Ten* was clearly etched in my brain. We each carried powerful searchlights for visibility in the channel. Silence prevailed. Suddenly, out of nowhere, two giant eagles appeared and began circling above *Precious Metal*.

"That means good luck according to First Nations culture!" I screamed with excitement. We all gazed at the two gliding eagles with incredulity.

The eagles' visit was short-lived and they disappeared as quickly as they had arrived. Suddenly *Precious Metal* released from the ocean floor and swung her bow directly into the wind. Did the eagles know the danger we were facing? What were they doing flying overhead in total darkness at 2.00 in the morning? Are they truly perceptive and more instinctive then we think?

I quickly engaged the engine. In complete darkness we cautiously manoeuvred *Precious Metal* towards *Ten* using radar and our intensely bright spotlights. Strong wind gusts and rain challenged us as we navigated our way towards the channel entrance. It took all of my navigational skills and concentration to bring *Precious Metal* safely alongside *Ten*.

Our elation and adrenalin rush kept us all awake until sunrise. The relief experienced by everyone on both boats was enormous. *Precious Metal* would survive to sail another day. It has been said that you're not a real sailor until you've grounded at least once. Nonetheless, I will always be mystified by the vigilant soaring eagles that suddenly appeared as our providers of good fortune in the final minutes before *Precious Metal* swung freely at precisely 2.00am.

The Whales

Several wonderful weeks of terrific guests and exciting exploration followed *Precious Metal's* infamous grounding experience. Our wise Kyuquot First Nations chief brought warm sunshine and temperatures for the entire final three weeks of the voyage. As we ventured further south we encountered more developed tourist surroundings, allowing Jane and me to part ways knowing that assistance was nearby in any emergency.

Angelo and I set sail from Hot Springs Cove early one morning, and immediately after exiting the bay a huge blanket of thick fog rolled in from the west and descended over *Precious Metal*. Angelo promptly became nauseous due to monstrous west coast swells and nestled into the cockpit corner, bravely displaying his green sea-sick appearance. The fog was so thick that I couldn't see *Precious Metal's* bow, forcing me to rely entirely on my radar for the entire 20-mile voyage.

The dense fog did not lift for the entire eight-hour journey, requiring intense concentration and fixation on the radar screen. Even more challenging was my awareness that a huge reef protrudes out of the entrance to Tofino Harbour, and without visibility I could be in serious trouble. My adrenalin mounted as I heard Tofino's fog bell chime from a distance and it became louder as I approached the rocky shoreline. If only the fog would lift even slightly! Finally, I gathered my courage. Surrounded by total whiteness, I blindly turned towards the invisible Tofino lighthouse, the existence of which was determined solely by radar and sound.

Splash! Suddenly a gigantic humpback whale emerged out of the whiteness and breached within six feet of *Precious Metal's* port beam. This startling creature sent *Precious Metal* rocking profusely and woke Angelo from his deep slumber. The whale was enormous and began swimming alongside us as we watched in amazement. As soon as the tumultuous waves from the whale settled, another equally gigantic humpback whale emerged on our starboard side! Both whales began swimming towards the Tofino entrance with *Precious Metal* sandwiched in between. I had no escape.

While I always practised keeping 100-metre distance from any whale sighting, this scenario was unique. Angelo and I decided to maintain our course with the whales since they seemed to have a navigational advantage in the fog. Did they sense my concern about entering the bay and decide to guide us through the hazardous channel? Equally amazing was how they successfully led us through a narrow pass to the anchorage and disappeared as soon as we were safely in the bay.

A number of wonderful guests continued to join *Precious Metal* for the balance of her Vancouver Island circumnavigation including my three very special girlfriends: Joanne Vickery, Del Eckstein and Wendy Whiting. I'm forever grateful to everyone who devoted their holiday towards my epic virgin voyage and cherish the many fond memories. Spiritually, if I hadn't witnessed the eagle and whale experiences myself, I would be inclined to challenge their authenticity. Instead, I gained remarkable respect for these creatures. Their innate instincts are truly daunting.

CHAPTER 3

Girls' Night

November 2005

WELL GIRLS, I have an announcement to make," I said, gaining my courage after a huge gulp of red wine. Our Wednesday 'girls' night' pot-luck ritual was hosted at Joanne's glamorous home. We had just finished dinner and settled into comfortable chairs on her back deck overlooking Semiahmoo Bay which borders British Columbia (Canada) and Washington State (United States). Before I could retract my previous sentence, I blurted out, "I'm moving to Port Hardy."

Silence. Wendy, Joanne and Del became spellbound and in unison reached for their wine glass. Awestruck and wide-eyed, one-by-one they assembled their composure and stared blankly towards me. I now had centre stage.

While I've been blessed to have so many wonderful friends in my life, these girls have been like sisters to me. We always laughed about writing a best-selling screenplay or novel based on our incredible times together. Most recently, they had kept me propped up and positive through my entire separation and divorce. In addition to the memorable fun times, we had also individually experienced monumental lifetime challenges together – as four dynamic, fit, successful women (and mothers) facing the inevitable implications of becoming middle-aged. We could always count on each other for support and never made judgements.

"You're moving to where, Pamela?" asked Wendy, who is always so thoughtful and diplomatic. "Port Hardy. That tiny coastal town on the northern end of Vancouver Island. Remember I sailed there last summer and really liked it?" Sheepishly I continued, "Do you think we should uncork another bottle of wine for this one?" Silently, they all nodded in unison. I leapt into action and ran to the kitchen attempting to keep my composure. Hearing me voice my new plans out loud made them suddenly seem so real. This called for an extra special vintage of wine.

"It just seems like the right decision for me," I explained as I topped up each of their glasses. "First, that region offers an exceptional coastline for my new charter business. It's pristine, really beautiful in the summers and full of nature's best marine life and wildlife. Not only are the magnificent Broughton Islands on the doorstep of Port Hardy, but the 300 miles northwards to the Canada/Alaska border encompasses the protected Great Bear Rainforest and the entire region is virtually untouched. There are so many fabulous places to explore and share with my charter guests. Operating my charter business based from Port Hardy would be so unique and exciting."

"There's another attraction which I haven't told you about. Remember last summer when I was there for six days between guests on my circumnavigation around Vancouver Island?" They all nodded, perplexed and intrigued.

"The owner of the marina is named Ilver Villani. He's Italian and seems like a super nice man. As you know, I've dated a ton of guys here in the city and none have caught my attention. Ilver seems so genuine, caring, fun and he's a successful businessman. Something about him is really attractive to me. Ever since I met him last summer we've emailed and stayed in touch. Anyway, he called me yesterday knowing my intentions of starting a charter business and said that the existing charter company in Port Hardy is leaving and there's room for me to work out of his marina. I'll be the only sailing charter business in that region."

The discussion became more intense as we all weighed the

pros and cons of leaving the city and the many amenities I enjoy: squash, skiing, yacht clubs, so many friends, as well as my ongoing chairmanship of the Victoria to Maui Yacht Race. "You realize you'll have to make big changes to your fancy wardrobe, sexy car, sophisticated dining and so much more," said Del, who always exhibited the trendiest persona. "Sure," I replied defensively. "That's crossed my mind, but I lived in the Yukon for 10 years so I know what to expect from small, remote communities."

"What about us? This changes the dynamics of our foursome?" asked Joanne in a sombre tone. "I know, Joanne. I've thought about it a lot as well. Also, my squash buddies who I adore so much and so many others. I know I'm leaving a lot behind. Yet, I'm only a day away and I'll keep my home here until it's certain that I want to move there. There's even a squash club in the town and a small ski facility an hour away. Plus, you won't believe this, but my captain's licensing course is being offered in Port McNeil, which is only a 40-minute drive away and starts in March – perfect timing! I have to obtain my Master Captain's License to operate the charter business. Essentially, it's an exciting new beginning for me and since my new life is about following my heart, it seems like a wonderful blend of business, romance and pleasure."

"Pamela, it sounds like you're already convinced, so let's toast to your new beginning," said Wendy.

"Our next girls' trip is to Port Hardy!" exclaimed Joanne. "I'll help you decorate your new home!" cried Del.

"Oh girls, I'm going to miss you so much!" I cried. We all came together with a big hug as tears gently rolled down each of our cheeks.

As I drove home that evening, the reality of my decision began to sink in. I didn't hear a thumbs-up or a thumbs-down from my girlfriends. "Pamela, what are you thinking?" Yet my heart said that it was the right decision – although where it would lead was a complete mystery.

Before I knew it, I had said my good-byes to many wonderful friends. *Precious Metal*, Riley and I were bound for one of Canada's last frontiers and beginning a new adventure. Early February, during the heart of winter, we fought the rain, wind, fog, currents and humongous waves as we gunk-holed northbound along the formidable BC coastline 300 nautical miles to Port Hardy – which subsequently became our home for the following five years.

On a sunny day, there are few places on the planet as magical as Port Hardy. *Precious Metal* arrived unscathed and nestled into her B dock birth at the Quarterdeck Marina under bright clear skies. Instantly she, Riley and I became the new spectacle in the tiny town of less than 5,000 people. Rumours began that the new blue boat belonged to "Ilver's girlfriend" which became my identity; in fact, for the longest time I wondered if anyone even knew my name?

CHAPTER 4

Port Hardy

March 2006

I T WASN'T UNTIL the first session of my Master's Captain's License that I fully appreciated the meaning of culture shock and its drastic impact on my new transition to Port Hardy. In typical fashion I carefully selected my attire for my first Captain's License theory class with the notion I did not want to appear overdressed but keeping in mind my mother's dictum: we don't have a second chance to make a good first impression. Grooming and the right 'look' in fashion was indoctrinated into my psyche since childhood. For the first class meeting, I selected designer denim jeans, a smart custom-fit black leather jacket, a simple, but somewhat sexy silk blouse, low casual heels, a designer leather belt and complimentary neck scarf to pull the entire 'look' together. My French nails and highlighted hair were impeccable and I never left home without a tiny dash of my favourite Chanel No. 5 fragrance.

While I never intended to attract attention with my attire, I always tried to look my best everywhere I went. Since I would be meeting fellow boaters, I naturally imagined these new classmates would become my North Island boating friends – similar to my fellow members at the prestigious Royal Vancouver Yacht Club in the city. What was I thinking?

I arrived at the designated high school location ahead of schedule in my hot Crossfire sports car only to find the doors still locked. I anxiously waited in my car in anticipation of my fellow classmates' arrival. One by one I witnessed a sight to behold as their noisy, beaten-up old trucks approached the parking lot and they casually marched up the steps into the school. I had never witnessed such a motley-looking bunch of people. *Slightly overdressed, Pamela? Good grief...what were you thinking?* I wanted to escape but it was too late. Given that I was the only woman in the class, my instructor easily identified me, came to my car to introduce himself and ushered me into the classroom.

When I entered the classroom, one could have heard a pin drop. Twelve hard-core, tough-looking commercial fishermen and tug-boat operators stared at me incredulously. Talk about a fish out of water! Looking around, I noticed that our fingernails matched except that theirs were 'French black' filled with diesel oil and grime. Their clothes were disgustingly grubby, as if they had come directly from their commercial boats to attend class. My Chanel fragrance was drowned by their *Eau de fish* and diesel oil.

Not only was I the only woman, but I was a sailor – which made them even more suspicious of my status in this classroom. Generally, these groups of seamen despise sailors; we're too wimpy, environmentally sensitive and get in their way as they navigate the high seas in their large vessels. For the first time in my life I felt like the ultimate blonde bimbo. I even contemplated running next door and joining the Weight Watchers group in the adjacent classroom. *Oh, Pamela, how did you get this so wrong?*

Our instructor politely circled the room asking each student to briefly introduce themselves, providing a bit of background, previous boating experience and our reasons for taking the class. Over time, after hearing these men's credentials, it struck me that I was in the midst of some of the most competent seamen on the planet. What an opportunity to learn from these people and hear their sea stories! *Just don't sit too close.* Ultimately I regained my composure and opened my mind to these tough, hearty men.

Undoubtedly, if I had taken this course in the city I'd have been amongst a group of fair-weather boaters. These guys were the real thing! I became spellbound by their fortitude and the stories these men had to tell. I made a mental note: *never judge a book by its cover; and, Pamela, don't waste your Chanel in the subsequent classes!*

For the next three weeks of class instruction and dialogue, I was like a sponge soaking up my classmates' mesmerizing tales of the sea. "Why do we need these tide books and navigation aids?" asked one fellow. "If I need to know the tide I simply look at the shoreline. If I need to know the weather I look at the sky. I've been navigating these waters all my life so these stupid charts and navigation books are a waste of my time."

Despite the fact that they were incredibly competent seamen, several had a tough time passing the course – if they passed at all. The course content was designed by government officials in pristine office towers and demanded proper study habits that were totally foreign to these men. Taking the exam was even more foreign to some of them.

On exam day, everyone assembled in a large classroom. We were a group of approximately 100 candidates from around the region. The examiner explained the rules of the 90-minute written test and quietly disappeared from the room. Two-thirds' through the time allotment, I was in deep concentration, filling out the multiple choice section when I heard a familiar voice from the front of the class call out loud, "Pamela, do you know the answer to number 87?" Poor guy, I thought. He's likely never taken a government exam before and probably didn't realize that this behaviour is actually cheating!

I handily passed the exam as well as the additional required courses – just in the nick of time since my first official charter was only three weeks after my final test. Had I failed my Captain's License exam, my entire summer of booked charters would have had to be cancelled.

Port Hardy is aptly named; however, it should have been spelled 'Port Hearty' after the people who reside there. (A play on words, since it was named after Captain Hardy who discovered the region in the late 1700s.) Rich with abundant virgin forest for logging, active sport and commercial fishing, as well as significant mining opportunities, Port Hardy's history has been boom or bust. Sadly, I was there during a bust cycle.

When forestry, mining and fishing industries were thriving (as recently as 20 or so years prior), the town boasted several shopping centres, a movie theatre, four squash courts and close to 20,000 people. Sadly, the latest economic downturn seriously impacted many industry towns like Port Hardy whose population has now diminished to less than 5,000, with a skeleton infrastructure and very few amenities.

However, Mother Nature easily made up for the town's shortfalls. Majestic, often snow-capped mountains line the shoreline on both sides of Queen Charlotte Strait, which is the waterway between Vancouver Island and the British Columbia mainland. Having the good fortune of an abundance of hiking and biking trails as well as fishing, kayaking and world-renowned scuba diving areas, the North Island is an outdoor person's paradise. It's not uncommon to walk the pristine shoreline and see a bear, or a whale breeching in the bay or a flock of gigantic eagles soaring overhead. The area represents the best of Mother Nature – when it's not raining.

My relationship with Ilver continued to flourish and as time elapsed we purchased a beautiful home on the spectacular Storey's Beach in a relatively up-scale community outside of the town. I also grew to love and respect Ilver's traditional Italian family who readily accepted and embraced me into their lives.

Having owned and developed several businesses in Port Hardy dating back to the early 1970s, Ilver was a very big fish in a small town and highly respected within the community. Hence, as Ilver's new girlfriend, I enjoyed an instantaneous welcome, making it easy to get established and I soon considered this wonderfully hospitable community my home. Despite continued my passion for dancing, city friends, squash, yacht affiliations and sophisticated lifestyle, I was quite satisfied with my life during those early years in Port Hardy with Ilver.

CHAPTER 5

Precious Yacht Charters

September 2006

THE CONCEPT OF owning and operating a sailing charter business seemed almost too good to be true. In theory, I would be sailing my beautiful boat all summer long, in absolutely stupendous surroundings, with interesting guests from all over the world – and be paid for the privilege! What more could one ask for in a business? What was I thinking?

The reality was that every day for the entire summer I was the captain, cook and dishwasher (for three full meals per day) in addition to having to prepare and serve appetizers and be an engaging hostess. I also had to provision the boat, clean and do the laundry and assume the roles of mechanic, electrician, administrator and navigator. It was truly exhausting. Furthermore, because I was always so busy, everyone seemed to be having fun on the boat except me.

Despite the fact that I enjoyed so many wonderful guests, the workload involved in operating a full-service, high-end charter business was far too demanding for one person. Taking on crew made no sense because this person would utilize a profitable sleeping birth. Also, given such a short tourist season, the additional salary and associated daily costs would take away from my already meagre income.

Of the 109 charter guests during the life of Precious Yacht Charters, 108 were terrific and provided me with wonderful memories. Essentially my five- to seven-day high-end charters focused on the magical inlets of the Broughton Island Archipelago during 2006 and further north into the Great Bear Rainforest in 2007. I could devote an entire book to these charters because they were all outstanding experiences despite the tremendous amount of work. Three charters are worthy of mention because of the unique circumstances and the challenges they placed my seamanship.

The Kermode Bear Charter

Fielding charter inquiries is an onerous daily task because undoubtedly the prospective clients ask a lot of obscure questions that need to be answered thoroughly; yet very few of these clients ever end up in a booking. One day I received a request for information from a European agent suggesting that his client was intent on seeing a Kermode bear (aka 'spirit bear') – which is a rare, white pigmented black bear that resides primarily on the remote Princess Royal Island within the Great Bear Rainforest.

I responded enthusiastically as always, "Yes, these bears are within my sailing region; however, they are incredibly elusive. Sightings are not impossible, but are highly improbable. That said, I will endeavour to do my very best to ensure a Kermode bear sighting." I refrained from suggesting that we specialize in sailing, rather than bear watching because I, too, was keen to explore the possibility of viewing a Kermode bear. I didn't hold my breath for a positive reply.

Not only did the agent reply immediately, but he booked right away and paid a deposit for a week that was available in early September; it would be the last charter of the season.

What was I thinking? I committed to taking unknown guests into an unknown territory in search of an animal that I barely knew anything about! Needless to say, I subsequently researched every bit of information relating to these special bears and also contacted all available resources regarding their possible, but improbable whereabouts. At the time, my research indicated that approximately 55 of these animals existed on the planet. My stress level went into the stratosphere as I embarked on this final charter of the season.

By late August, I was totally exhausted from back-to-back charters throughout the summer season. So I hired a local Port Hardy woman named Noreen for this last Kermode bear charter to assist with cooking and clean up. Noreen had a great personality and since it was a two-person charter, there was space available for Noreen to sleep in the main salon.

Noreen arrived by commuter plane into my base community of Shearwater a day before our guests Maurice and Elsa arrived. I allowed this time to acquaint Noreen with the galley and do any last-minute provisioning. Remarkably, late that afternoon as we strolled along the sidewalk past the tiny local establishments, a woman in a small concession store was hanging up a short white fur coat in her showcase window!

I stopped in my tracks in front of the store window. "Noreen, we have to buy that coat! If we can't provide a true Kermode bear sighting by the final day of the charter, you can wear that coat and pretend to be a bear!" This was the only solution to my anguish of the possibility of not sighting a bear. Her questioning look of disbelief gradually turned into enthusiastic approval as she followed my train of thought.

We immediately entered the store and grabbed the white fur coat from the window. The cost was incidental and within seconds I was the proud owner of a fake white fur coat. The saleslady was overwhelmed. "Don't you want to even try it on??" was the last we heard as we hurried out of the store in fits of laughter. *Precious Metal* could now guarantee a Kermode bear sighting – albeit contrived. I was no longer anxious about this pending charter and my spirits were completely lifted.

Maurice and Elsa's flight arrived on schedule and after introductions and a customary safety review of the boat, I engaged the engine and explained, "The currents are in our favour for the next three hours and I have a lovely anchorage designated for this evening that I know you'll enjoy."

"Maurice, I thought you said that you hired a captain?" asked

Elsa. Silence followed. "I'm your captain," I replied hesitantly, having assumed that Maurice had apprised her of his charter arrangements beforehand, which entailed having a female captain. Any awkwardness was soon dispelled and *Precious Metal* set out on her final exciting charter of the season, with an engaging and enthusiastic couple who appeared to be in their late 60s.

My friends who had local knowledge of the Princess Royal Island region assured me of the exact location that Kermode bears were most likely to be seen – near the base of a certain waterfall at the very tip of Loredo Inlet. We arrived at our destination by mid-afternoon the following day. The routine for the next four days was to paddle the dinghy quietly up the far side of the river and wait. Patience and stillness would be a necessity.

Maurice happily complied and each day we set out to the same spectacular spot where giant eagles soared and an abundance of eager salmon were constantly swimming desperately up the river to their spawning grounds. Elsa, Noreen and Riley stayed aboard *Precious Metal* most days while Maurice and I ventured up the river in search of our prize.

On one occasion a grizzly bear and her two cubs sauntered along the opposite river bank and captured our scent. They each dug their own bed in the sand and watched us intently for what seemed like hours. Satisfied that we weren't a threat, they continued their search for dinner – happily swatting at the salmon with their giant paws and devouring them as if they were candy. In fact, the salmon were so plentiful and jumped so high around my dinghy, I was forced to swat them with my paddles as I manoeuvred the through the water.

One afternoon, I briefly left Maurice on the river bank and returned to *Precious Metal* to oversee the dinner plans. When I came back to retrieve him he had caught a salmon with his bare hands! His smile was larger than life and I'm confident that he'll be telling friends of his monumental fish tale until his grave. Needless to say, we feasted on his salmon that evening and I was ever hopeful that his 'fish story' alleviated some of his anxiety to view our treasured bear.

Finally, our day of reckoning was upon us. Despite every effort, after four intense days there was no sign of the infamous Kermode bear. Noreen and I shared an understanding nod at breakfast that morning. That day, on perhaps the hottest day of the summer, Noreen would turn herself into a white Kermode bear. We decided to take Maurice up the river one more time, while Elsa (who by this time was informed of our hoax) would help Noreen put on the bear costume. Fortunately, Noreen had matching white pants and a t-shirt. They skilfully sewed the hood of the coat tightly to wrap around Noreen's face. We were all very proud of our make-shift Kermode bear.

Our plan was to drop Noreen off at the mouth of the river. Elsa and I would continue up the river to meet Maurice in our dinghy. Noreen would then saunter in bear-fashion, along the shoreline towards us and eventually Maurice would experience the surprise of his life as he discovered his prize Kermode bear.

As planned, Noreen rolled out of the dinghy into some tall grass at the entrance of the river. After gathering herself, she sauntered along the shore as skilfully as if she had been a bear in her former life. It was one of the funniest sights of my lifetime. She did a four-legged run along the shore, stopped, pretended to sniff the surroundings, swatted a few salmon and continued to bumble along in a playful manner.

Elsa and I reached Maurice's location and secured the dinghy on the riverbank. We had to force ourselves to look away from Noreen because she was simply too hilarious to watch and we needed to be quiet. Maurice's attention was focused on some distant eagles and didn't notice Noreen as she continued to approach him. Soon our bear became impatient and began shaking tree branches and throwing rocks into the water to get his attention. The entire scene was so comical, mostly because Maurice was absorbed by some eagles nesting and neglected to look along the shoreline.

Finally, in desperation and overheated inside her fur coat, Noreen sprung out towards us from behind a fallen log, bringing a tremendous climax to our extraordinary episode. Maurice was absolutely flabbergasted and delighted with our attempt to provide him with a Kermode bear sighting. What a terrific ending to an almost impossible situation; and it allowed me to fulfil my company's motto: "Precious Yacht Charters guarantees to surpass our clients' expectations." Mission accomplished.

As I sailed away from Shearwater I felt a strong sense of elation. I looked up and saw the small commuter plane carrying Maurice, Elsa and Noreen dip its wing above *Precious Metal*. I was in celebration mode because my entire charter season was now completed and every aspect of it had been an amazing experience. Two whales helped me celebrate as they swam right alongside *Precious Metal*. It was a glorious sunny day with a wonderful downwind breeze and perfect sailing conditions. The strong current was in my favour providing a speed of over nine knots. My favourite Bob Marley sailing music was blaring. I was in heaven.

My usual half-way anchorage and overnight stop between Shearwater and Port Hardy was in Hakai Inlet; however, I didn't want this magical day of sailing to end and contemplated continuing straight to Port Hardy. My calculations for the tide to change were also in my favour, allowing me to complete the 90-mile voyage after sunset. There would be a partially full moon and therefore I would likely have sufficient light to visually navigate the harbour if, by chance, I was delayed. What was I thinking?

What I didn't count on was a storm that was brewing ahead in the tenuous Queen Charlotte Sound. I sailed past the last option for a suitable anchorage at 2.00pm and I was therefore committed to finishing the next 30 miles to Port Hardy. Suddenly my elation turned to anguish.

The winds and currents did a complete reversal and were against me. As *Precious Metal* was enduring tumultuous seas, the engine suddenly died. I had not properly calculated my fuel allowance between tanks and needed to pump more fuel into the day tank I was drawing from. I was in a dangerous location in close proximity to many huge reefs. All sense of celebration instantly evaporated as I realized the seriousness of the situation at hand. Fortunately, I had mastered pumping fuel between tanks; however, the rolling seas made the experience akin to performing this task from inside a washing machine.

For the next six hours *Precious Metal* bashed her way into huge steep seas in an effort to cross the notoriously challenging Strait. Finally, at approximately 10.00pm I entered a more protected group of islands. My night was not over. The full moon was not present because of the overcast skies. In complete darkness I was forced to navigate through the narrow Bates Passage. My penalty for error would be severe. Exhausted and completely focused on my radar, I managed to wind my way through the passage successfully in over 30 knots of wind. The anchorage retreat ahead of me in Port Alexandra was only 20 minutes away. *Stay focused, Pamela, you're nearly there.*

When I finally arrived at my destination, strong winds were howling and funnelling through Alexandra Bay. It took several tries to set my anchor securely. By 11.30pm I was finally safe and sound in a dark, stormy anchorage. I sadly looked at my dog and said, "Riley, my darling, I apologize but I won't be taking you to shore this evening. You'll just have to wait until early tomorrow morning." My last recollection of that evening was sipping both halves of my well-deserved celebratory McCallan single malt scotch in one sitting.

What was I thinking? I could have enjoyed a wonderful afternoon in my trusted Hakai Inlet anchorage and easily sailed to Port Hardy the following morning. Instead I pushed myself into a seriously tenuous situation. Stormy weather, fatigue and darkness are a recipe for disaster for a single-hander. It appears that the Sailing Gods were determined to test me to the very end of my charter season.

An Exciting Charter with BBC

I thought it was going to be an ordinary and tedious six-hour journey traveling from Vancouver to Port Hardy. Two-thirds through the ferry ride across Georgia Strait from Vancouver to Vancouver Island my cell phone rang with a call that made my heart jump. "Pamela, it's Bill on my radio phone from God's Pocket Resort. How would you like to do a BBC charter to Triangle Island?"

"Are you kidding?" I replied. "Of course I'd love to!" "I don't have any more details for you, but I'll get the guy to call you. You'll likely hear from him this afternoon," he said. That was the end of the phone conversation. "Cool," I replied, but he had already disengaged the call.

During my four-hour drive up the long and winding highway to Port Hardy, my mind raced between wondering if it was a joke, to what little I knew about Triangle Island. I knew that it was a protected marine reserve that was restricted from humans except for a few privileged researchers who study its indigenous rare species of birds and marine life. I also knew that Triangle Island was a long, long way out to sea from the formidable Cape Scott at the very far end of the Scott Island chain. Not wanting to miss the phone call forced my pedal to the metal. I was exhilarated to say the least.

Within minutes of entering my home, the phone rang. "This is Hugh from BBC in Oxford, England. Is this Pamela?" I had to pull myself off the ceiling (*stay cool, Pamela*). His sexy British voice had me convinced that I was speaking with the film star Hugh Grant! He asked me a few questions regarding my seamanship and qualifications which all filled his expectations. We discussed the details of his charter proposal. Not only was I able to schedule the charter, but the crew and camera equipment were arriving the following week!

He apologized (in a coy Hugh Grant manner) for such short notice, explaining that it took our various government agencies extensive time to approve their application to embark on the Island and they couldn't coordinate the charter arrangements until they had a permit. "Absolutely no problem," I replied, still enthralled with the concept that I was speaking with Hugh Grant. He could have told me my house was burning down and I would have responded in the same manner.

The documentary on Triangle Island was a segment of a

BBC feature entitled, *Nature's Great Events* which was the sequel to the award winning documentary *Planet Earth*. The event in the case of Triangle Island relates to plankton and the series of Earth's amazing events in nature that take place when the ocean's plankton bloom. Triangle Island is the second largest Steller sea lion rookery in the world (among many other unique species) and the production crew were hoping to capture birth of baby seal lion pups as well as the natural evolution and dependency of all other species that rely on and develop subsequent to the plankton blooming.

It all happened so quickly. The only negotiating discussion was about the duration of the charter. Hugh envisioned that we would only need one week to accomplish the filming. I warned him that the weather in that area could be nasty in June and I recommended that even two weeks was questionable to obtain the sunshine they needed during filming. He finally agreed to two weeks.

Before I had time to digest the magnitude of this two-week charter, the papers were signed and faxed back and forth between me and their various legal and sundry departments. The charter was confirmed and paid for by dinner time.

What was I thinking? As I attempted to fall asleep that night the reality of the day's commitment began to consume me. It occurred to me that the reason Precious Yacht Charters was chosen was because no other local charter company wanted to take it! The coastline of the Island was surrounded by rugged reefs and the weather at that time of year could be horrid. From my brief research, only one anchorage existed, which was south facing, and the nasty storms came from the south in June. In trepidation, I'm not sure if I slept again for the following week and I worked solidly on the boat throughout each and every day in preparation for this exciting adventure – including buying and installing a new offshore commercial life raft.

After my third consecutive sleepless night that week I realized that I was clearly over my head with this charter and I would be wise to have at least one crew to help with the logistics of getting the film crew to shore as well as any boat challenges that could occur in such a remote setting. I sent a handful of competent friends a synopsis of the pending charter and within an hour of my email my friend, Roger Elmes, responded positively. Roger was a Canadian Navy veteran and owned the 65-foot McGregor sailboat that I helped crew as navigator in the 1992 Victoria to Maui Yacht Race. Having recently retired as Dean of British Columbia's Kwantlen University, Roger was available to promptly arrive in Port Hardy as needed the following week.

The BBC film crew consisted of two people: the producer named Ed Charles who appeared to be in his late 20s, and a highly reputable photographer, Gavin Thurston, who had a 40-something look about him. Both men seemed very personable and had obviously worked together on many prior occasions. They and their 1,000 pounds of camera equipment arrived as scheduled on June 2. A helicopter was organized to fly them and their gear to Triangle Island on June 4.

Their intention was to camp in tents and film for two weeks on the southern side of the Island where there's just enough usable space for a small research hut and two tiny tents. My charter was to begin on June 16 when they wanted to film the eastern side of the island, which is the location of the sea lion rookery and only accessible by water.

During one of our introductory meetings they jokingly advised me that I was speaking on the phone with a man named Hugh Pearson and not Hugh Grant. We all had a good laugh over my naive misconception.

Every square inch of the helicopter was utilized to pack Ed, Gavin and their gear – including the sizeable pontoon compartments. As I waved farewell, and their helicopter vanished into the sky, my favourite song, *Over the Rainbow*, was playing on my car radio. This became my theme song for the charter, because at this juncture in my life all of my dreams were coming true.

I was able to stay in contact with Ed and Gavin by satellite phone and shortly after their arrival onto a very stormy Triangle

Island they notified me that they needed more supplies. They arranged another helicopter trip for the following week to transport these necessities (and some scotch!) and offered me the chance to fly in the helicopter. In this case, I could view the Island by air, see the available anchorages, reefs and hazards, as well as observe by air whether the sea lions inhabited the eastern side as predicted.

Skirting the entire rugged North Island coastline was an awesome ride. The outcrops of rocky reefs surrounding the Island appeared fiercer than I had previously envisioned. I was only able to visit my team for the short time that it took to unload the helicopter; however, I did manage to see their primitive environment and share a few fun moments together.

Triangle Island is aptly named because the contour of the Island, as well as the rugged surrounding outcrops, are all weathered into the shapes of triangles. The Island has an long history and once had a lighthouse at the top – 800 feet above sea level – which was eventually dismantled because it was commonly in the clouds and rarely visible. Many people and experienced local fishermen warned me of Triangle Island's treacherous weather and dangerous surrounding reefs in the weeks leading to my upcoming charter.

Customary with all charters I asked Ed, Gavin and Roger whether they had any food restrictions or preferences. They all seemed to be low maintenance, although Gavin did comment that, "You can serve me hot dogs for every meal, but all I ask for is a good cup of coffee in the morning." Needless to say, I bought the best coffee that money could buy and was satisfied that my menus would far surpass their expectations of hot dogs.

As scheduled, Roger and I departed Port Hardy early morning on June 15 bound for Hope Island, 20 nautical miles north and a good departure point for the 30-mile stretch to Triangle Island the following day. My final long-term weather report for Triangle Island was not favourable and was haunting me as I headed *Precious Metal* over the infamous Nahwitti Bar and out to sea. As we passed Cape Scott and navigated our way through the stunning Scott Islands towards Triangle Island, the skies became darker and darker. A strong weather system was forming from the south – which was exactly what I feared.

Our reception by Ed and Gavin into the southern anchorage was monumental, as they stood on the shore looking like abandoned refugees finally awaiting their rescue. Roger managed to retrieve them from shore in the dinghy amongst huge crashing waves and safely brought them aboard *Precious Metal*. They each downed two cold beers as they shared their remarkable stories of their previous two weeks living in their tents and trying to film in the worst storms that they had ever experienced. It must have been a formidable ordeal since these brave men have filmed in precarious places all over the world.

As I listened to their entertaining conversation, my eyes were focusing on the storm building behind us, which was rapidly moving closer. This was no anchorage to be in during a storm. "I'm so incredibly sorry guys, but I'm afraid that a storm is approaching and this party is over. Roger needs to take you to shore immediately and we have to leave." With two six-packs in hand they immediately departed and Roger was back aboard instantly.

We had no sooner weighed our anchor than a harrowing gale of 35 knots was upon us. It was all I could do to safely drive *Precious Metal* into clearance beyond the reefs. For the next four hours we were pounded with beam seas, huge vertical swells and the storm was relentless. By 7.00pm *Precious Metal* was safely anchored in a cove behind a tiny Scott Island that a local fisherman had recommended. We were safe for the night; however, the winds relentlessly screeched through the rigging until dawn. We headed back to Port Hardy the following day. The subsequent storms on Triangle Island were so intense that it was another six days before the weather would cooperate enough to re-visit Ed and Gavin. They must have been really impressed – paying for a full-week charter and all we had provided was two beers, two six-packs and a one-hour visit. At least they had been warned.

Roger and I anchored at Hope Island overnight on Day 7 and managed to find clear weather during our day-long passage back to Triangle Island. By satellite phone, I advised Ed and Gavin to have all of their camera equipment and belongings ready for our 2.00pm arrival. My intentions were to get in and out of the Island as quickly as possible and back to Hope Island by darkness to avoid being exposed to yet another storm. Everything succeeded as planned.

Finally on Day 10 we awoke to sunshine. We departed the Hope Island anchorage at sunrise and arrived at our anchorage on the eastern side of Triangle Island by mid-afternoon. It was a sight and experience that adjectives simply don't describe.

The noise from the Island was deafening as though we were anchored alongside a motorcar speedway. Over 1,000 sea lions located on a stretch of beach that was approximately the size of a football field were making ghastly noises – all at the top of their lungs. Their putrid scent was my second sense to be aroused. A number of large sea lions curiously swam by *Precious Metal*. The entire commotion was spellbinding. Given that sunset was at approximately 10.00pm, we immediately prepared the necessary gear for the first step of many in the task of photography: establishing blinds from the furthest access point to the beach.

My first photography lesson from these experts was that one simply doesn't descend on the subjects. Building blinds at regular intervals along the shoreline is a lengthy and tedious process so that the animals are never spooked or aware of your presence. Once the blinds are established, the team quietly moves themselves and the gear forward to the subsequent blinds until they are in downwind proximity for photos. It can take half a day to cross half of the space of a football field and we would often need to climb along the hillside to avoid being noticed by the sea lions. Nature photographers of this calibre need to be in terrific shape to manoeuvre the equipment and themselves in these precarious settings.

Roger and I took turns staying on the boat and tending the dinghy for the following two days. My most thrilling sequence of events was watching a birth of a baby sea lion from behind a blind, six feet away. As well, I watched a bull kill his pup, taking

A curious Steller sea lion bull, with Precious Metal *at anchor near Triangle Island*

it into his mouth and with one wicked motion throwing it into the sea water. He must have been bad! Witnessing the splendid talent of these men who are instinctively cognisant of exactly when to photograph was thrilling. I truly learned to appreciate what it takes behind the scenes to make a quality documentary of this calibre.

At night, once we were fed, Ed and Gavin worked tirelessly to review and edit their day's material. My nightly task was to grind the coffee beans with a rolling pin because I forgot to bring a proper grinder for Gavin's one-and-only request for a good cup of coffee! What was I thinking? We also listened to their many exhilarating tales of their worldwide experiences in film making. Gavin is world renowned in photography and spent many years as David Attenborough's protégé all over the world. Mostly, they were tons of fun and such a treat to have aboard. I felt extremely privileged to have the opportunity to spend such quality time together.*

On our 14th and last day of the charter the skies became overcast, which was not conducive to photography; besides, they were confident that their footage from the few available working days was superb. We decided to abandon Triangle Island and

This huge humpback whale performed a show for us and then dove directly underneath Precious Metal

head back to Port Hardy. During this voyage a huge humpback whale decided to display its talents and began breaching adjacent to *Precious Metal*. We all brought out our cameras. Roger took the helm while Ed, Gavin and I were on *Precious Metal*'s top deck. Suddenly the humpback turned and dove directly under the amidships of the boat. I inadvertently screamed, "Holy Shit!"

"Is that a nautical term?" asked Gavin smugly with his British humour.

"Yes, and I'm confident it isn't the first or last time I'll be using it," I replied.

As we motored into Hardy Bay for our final time I played *Over the Rainbow* on my stereo and we all embraced in a huge hug together with tears streaming from our eyes. I was well aware that these types of monumental experiences rarely pass through our lives. This charter had been an incredible privilege.

---

* I continue to stay in touch with both Ed and Gavin from the BBC charter. During a recent lunch with Ed and Gavin in Bristol, England (March 2012) Gavin had just finished filming the next award-winning documentary Frozen Planet, *with David Attenborough. Ed continues to work in the film industry.*

Charter #109: North to Alaska

My final charter happened unexpectedly during a short 10-day break that I had intentionally planned mid-summer in order to have an opportunity to relax and enjoy the surrounding areas of Port Hardy. I was enjoying a festive beach party with local friends when my cell phone rang at 8.30pm. The caller was frantic. He was an American who owned a sailing charter business in Alaska and had hit a rock earlier that day on his sailboat causing major damage and losing his keel. "Pamela, I desperately need someone to take my guests from Ketchikan, Alaska, to Juneau next week. They're friends of mine and I can't let them down. Do you know of anyone who can do this?" We exchanged a few more details and I wrote the phone number of the guests in the sand. Given that I had the time and always wanted to sail to Alaska, I phoned the pending guests and shortly thereafter, to my surprise, I had booked the charter – bound for Alaska at 6.00am the following morning.

What was I thinking? I had skeleton charts for certain sections in the northern British Columbia region, minimal food aboard and in order to arrive on schedule the following Tuesday I would have to cover 80 miles each day, which I knew would be exhausting. Furthermore, I had done absolutely no preparation for a voyage single-handedly that many people take a lifetime to plan. Needless to say, my festivities at the beach party abruptly halted and I immediately began preparing for my northbound 400-mile solo adventure to Alaska.

Although tiresome, every day of my voyage featured spectacular scenery and magical surroundings as I ventured through the Inland Passage which boasts stunning snow-capped mountain peaks and heavily forested coastal terrain. My diet consisted of popcorn, peanut butter and granola bars. I was famished when I finally arrived into Prince Rupert at 9.30pm on my third night of the voyage. The light of Smiley's Seafood Diner shone brightly above the marina and after securing my dock lines I frantically raced up the hill arriving two minutes before their 10.00pm closing time. "Please ask the chef for the biggest hamburger he has in stock and top it with every food group imaginable," I said to the waitress. "I haven't eaten a proper meal in three days." She promptly placed my order and to this day, I have never devoured a hamburger with such an appreciation and satisfaction. Smiley made me very smiley.

My guests, consisting of a family of four from the United States, were waiting for me as scheduled at the dock in Ketchikan waving their arms in anticipation of my arrival. After brief introductions and pleasantries we provisioned the boat with food and I purchased the necessary charts for our upcoming voyage. By nightfall we were all keen and well prepared for our six-day adventure to Juneau.

Sometimes life just doesn't seem fair. Despite our best intentions we awoke to intense rain and overcast skies, which didn't abate for the entire voyage. My guests never saw a mountain, glacier, whale, iceberg – in fact they barely saw the coastline with exception to our evening anchorages. It was such a disappointment for all concerned. In addition to several remote anchorages, we stopped in the charming seaside fishing villages of Wrangell and Petersburg; however, the family could barely leave the boat because of the blistering rain. Most of our days were spent motoring through the narrow channels, massive icebergs and heavy traffic using the radar for navigation, while the family resorted to playing card games and reading in stormy, wet and cold conditions.

My final docking in Juneau was the most spectacular of my lifetime. I radioed ahead to the port captain asking for a docking space and after determining the size of my boat he kindly offered to place me on the cruise ship dock. I thanked him profusely imagining a long, extended dock with plenty of room. What was I thinking? As we approached the dock, I didn't expect to find two gigantic cruise ships moored bow-to-bow allowing minimal room for *Precious Metal*. When I radioed him a second time he replied, "There's 50 feet between the bow of the cruise ships, I paced it out myself." I continued to maintain that there didn't appear to be 50 feet of clearance, but he insisted there was enough room.

"Great," I said to my guests. "I not only have an opportunity to hit not one but two cruise ships today, but it's cocktail hour and all of the guests are on their balconies. We'll have an audience of about 4,000 people watching us!" I instructed everyone to hold on tightly and placed the two children inside the boat while the parents were given the docking lines and explicit directions for landing. Against strong wind and currents I directed *Precious Metal* between the massive ships and gunned the throttle in forward gear. The winds were too strong to gently idle forward.

At the precise critical moment when I was in perfect alignment with the cruise ships, I turned the steering wheel hard to port and spun *Precious Metal* 90 degrees to a full stop along the dock. It took us all several seconds to digest this flawless manoeuvre. No one was more shocked and pleasantly surprised as me! The dock master dutifully took my lines and congratulated me. Most revealing was my realization that I could handle *Precious Metal* in the direst circumstances. While I would always hold the highest respect for Mother Nature and the oceans, my apprenticeship as *Precious Metal*'s new captain was completed and I was ready to take on the challenges of offshore sailing to tropical regions.

Ironically, almost the minute after my guests' departure the following morning, the sun began to shine with not a cloud in the sky. During my six-day voyage back to Port Hardy I witnessed huge icebergs, spectacular glaciers, magnificent mountain ranges, fabulous whale shows, a fascinating wolf kill, terrific winds for sailing – essentially the very best of Alaska's natural beauty – and not a drop of rain.

CHAPTER 6

Preparing Precious Metal for Offshore

August 2008

I T'S FORTUITOUS THAT I didn't know what I didn't know about boat mechanics, maintenance and repairs as I was preparing for my offshore adventure. Because I know that if I knew what I didn't know, I likely would not have considered this voyage; and I wouldn't have experienced this monumental adventure.

The preparations required in actually sailing *Precious Metal* were the least of my worries. I was comfortable with navigation as well as being at sea for endless days. Thankfully, I have never suffered from seasickness and believed I have always had the fortitude to carry on in the face of adversity. That said, I'm astounded at myself and often have laughed when I consider how blatantly naive and unaware I was about the magnitude of ongoing mechanical and maintenance skills required to keep a 50,000 pound vessel safe and seaworthy.

Precious Metal was constructed with very high-end mechanical equipment and electronic instrumentation. Why would it fail? Secondly, I had always hired skilled people to oversee my engine room and perform the mechanical and electrical repairs when needed; therefore, I really didn't know the extent of the work that they accomplished. I simply wrote them a cheque when the job was completed. I was too busy during my career to pay attention to what I call 'blue' (male) tasks aboard my boat.

That said, I did manage to take one hour out of my busy schedule to meet with the Ernie (the owner of the company that installed my 100 horsepower Isuzu engine), in order to learn everything I needed to know about this very important part of my boat. Ernie kindly granted me the time; although, in hindsight, what can you teach a blonde female about an engine in one short hour that would normally take most people (usually men) a lifetime to learn and process? What was I thinking? Ernie was extremely patient and cordial and thoroughly explained the oil dip stick and alternator (which I already knew), so following my one hour consultation I was unrealistically confident that I understood the workings of the entire engine.

"Will I need some spare parts?" I asked.

"Most definitely," Ernie said. "I think you'll need a thermostat."

"Why?" I asked curiously.

"Because if you're out in the ocean and your thermostat goes you'll be in big trouble," he replied.

I asked where this important thermostat is located on the engine and once he showed me, I was satisfied that I had it handled. "How many should I take?"

He suggested that I only needed one at $135.00.

"Perfect," I replied.

Ernie arranged for the purchase of my thermostat and I happily departed his store completely satisfied that my knowledge of engine maintenance was completed, carrying a tiny plastic bag containing my two-inch square thermostat back to the boat.

In hindsight, I commend Ernie for his wonderful sense of humour. Now, five years later, after obtaining a lot of new mechanical wisdom, I have a comprehensive compartment of spare engine parts under my queen-size bunk that occupies the entire space – three feet deep – and amounts to several thousands of dollars. What I find particularly amusing is that every six months I do my spare parts inventory and each time I complete the task I record "one thermostat". It's the only spare part that I've never needed! (I would like to know what Ernie was thinking during his hour meeting with this dizzy blonde who intended to go offshore knowing absolutely nothing about engines.)

Subsequent to my meeting with Ernie was my confrontation with the boat heater repair man named Rob. On two occasions I asked him to fix my diesel heater and on both occasions he responded by email with the same comment, "Pamela, your diesel is dirty and needs to be cleaned."

"Don't worry about my diesel, just fix my furnace!" I responded angrily on both occasions. Exasperated with Rob, I finally gave up dealing with him and decided to abandon the idea of fixing my furnace since I was planning to head to the tropics and hopefully wouldn't need it. It took me two years of tinkering in the engine room before the light suddenly came on in my brain. Now I get it! You can't run a diesel furnace with dirty diesel. What was I thinking? I feel like such an idiot for getting angry with Rob – I simply didn't get it.

Having never been raised in a mechanical environment, tools opened up an entire new world for me. Fortunately *Precious Metal* has always been well equipped with tools; I just never knew what they were for. I did know about screwdrivers, the hammer and pliers. I didn't know anything about socket wrenches, drills, vice grips, hose clamps and the myriad of different types of screws, nuts and bolts and their applications. I even have a drill press aboard which I conveniently use as a terrific hat holder. Truthfully, I've only turned on my drill press once and it scared me to death so I've never used it since.

It has taken me years to learn when and how to use the tools I own. I have uniquely different names for each of my tools including the 'upside-down' socket screwdriver – which I usually have to use when I'm in that position. Also, having to learn about various types of wrenches, different lubricants, thread binders, solvents, cleaners, strippers, rust treatments, (and much more) has been a huge eye-opener. Again, I simply didn't know what I didn't know and it's a very good thing!

On my final week before my departure from Port Hardy I was frantically busy organizing the boat, safety equipment, food provisions and my crew logistics. *Precious Metal*'s home in Port Hardy had always been moored on B dock at the Quarterdeck Marina and throughout the three years my fellow boat owners on that dock had become notable friends. B dock was comprised of unique characters that one could easily include in a television sitcom. You couldn't make these people up! They came from a variety of backgrounds and were always happy to greet me on the dock – not to mention share some laughs over a few beers and sea stories as we all simultaneously worked on our boats. It was a special environment which I will always cherish.

Yet, that final week was more intensely emotional as we all began to realize that *Precious Metal* would soon be gone. Each afternoon Mick, Marty, Al, Tina and a number of local sports fishermen friends would bring their folding chairs and beer coolers alongside *Precious Metal*'s dockside location and essentially assist in commandeering my last-minute decisions about what to put where.

I will always remember my final afternoon when my last challenge was to find a bracket for securing my outboard engine on the back rail. Mick immediately produced a 2x4 plank of wood from his boat which we painted dark blue to match my boat and secured it on the rail. Despite the paint fading and the wood disintegrating over the years, that plank has sailed with me throughout the voyage as my memorable treasure from B dock.

After an emotional farewell and extending their very best wishes, my B dock buddies departed with their folding chairs and coolers for the very last time. *Precious Metal* and I were left alone to contemplate this huge new chapter that we were embarking on. Where will it take us? What would my life be like for the next few years? Is *Precious Metal* truly ready for her next adventure? What have I forgotten to do? What will become of me?

I closed my hatches and walked down the dock with bitter-sweet emotions, knowing that tomorrow would be the very first day of our new lives. My life as I knew it would be drastically changing. The following morning *Precious Metal*, Riley and I would be departing Port Hardy at sunrise and sailing 300 miles south to Vancouver where I would be picking up my crew and doing last-minute provisioning before heading south along the formidable west coast of North America to San Diego.

Leaving Port Hardy was also an important new phase in terms of my relationship with Ilver. During our final dinner we made plans for his pending visit to Vancouver a week later. He would be joining a special group of my friends at a final farewell party at the Royal Vancouver Yacht Club where I had been a member for many years. Our future intentions were that Ilver would continue to finish his development project in Port Hardy and join me periodically at special, interesting locations throughout my voyage. At the time it seemed like a heavenly solution that accommodated both of our business and sailing aspirations.

I awoke at 6.00am to the early morning fog that Port Hardy is notorious for in August. We all scrambled to assemble my bags hoping that the fog would lift, but it didn't. Once everything was aboard *Precious Metal* and my 7.00am departure was upon us, I gave Ilver a huge hug and cast my dock lines from B dock for the very last time. The fog was so thick that I was totally surrounded by whiteness – as though I was in a huge blanket of cotton. Sadly, without visibility, I remember thinking that I never really had a chance to properly say good-bye to the town. Instead, my eyes were focused on my radar as I slowly crept out of the bay.

Two hours later the fog lifted and the wind began to accumulate behind me. I hoisted all of my sails and experienced an incredibly exhilarating and breath-taking sail through the snow-capped mountains of Johnstone Strait. *Precious Metal* began to sail in full gear – like a horse heading to its barn. She knew she was heading to her new destiny in the tropics and she performed as if she was embracing a new life. Rarely do the wind, currents and seas allow for such perfect conditions and that 10-hour day was a magical sailing experience that will live with me forever.

I made a few stops along my southbound voyage including Desolation Sound where I met up with wonderful friends – Adele and Andre aboard their boat *Julius C.* I also attempted

A glorious sail down Johnstone Strait during my final days in Canada

to stop in Powell River at Ilver's family's home; however, a huge tug boat and barge intercepted my path to their home. Finally, when it was obvious that I wouldn't be able to get past the barge, their entire family lined together on the hillside and waved a wonderful and meaningful farewell.

My long-time girlfriend Jennifer Villard joined me the following day in Pender Harbour. She and her husband Noel have been terrific friends since the 1970s. Jenny sailed with me the final leg of my trip to Vancouver which meant so much to me. At our final lunch she presented me with a parting gift of two huge Olympic flags from her Whistler community (that hosted the Olympics) which I continue to cherish and display proudly in every opportunity that arises.

Three very special friends enthusiastically agreed to accompany me from Vancouver to San Diego: Jim Grace, Guy Walters and Joanne Vickery. Jim and Guy were both experienced offshore sailors, while my girlfriend Joanne had recently obtained her sailing credentials by taking numerous courses. Knowing that Joanne was a terrific cook, I placed her in charge of our culinary department. I was excited to have such a competent and fun team for this inaugural voyage and was completely confident that this lifetime adventure was off to a magical beginning.

We scrambled all week long in Vancouver to load *Precious Metal* with the final list of provisions, Joanne's delicious prepared meals and necessary items that weren't available in Port Hardy. I also made a special effort to make the rounds to my squash club friends at the River Club, as well as my former office and so many other noteworthy people whom I had grown to love over the years.

Before I knew it our farewell party was under way. Our new exciting adventure was about to begin. Meaningful tears appeared in my eyes with each farewell embrace as my valued friends eventually departed that evening. I still remember the melancholy feeling that came upon me as I lay in my bunk that night. This is it – it's really happening. There's no looking back.

Section Two

Twenty years from now you'll be more disappointed by the things that you didn't do than by the ones you did. So throw off the bowline. Sail away from the safe harbour. Catch the trade winds in your sails. Explore. Dream. Discover.

MARK TWAIN

CHAPTER 7

Precious Metal's Shakedown Voyage

August 25, 2008

THE FIRST MAJOR ocean passage of a boat is referred to as a 'shakedown' voyage. This is an opportunity to discover any deficiencies, weaknesses, necessary upgrades and supplies in preparation for future ocean voyages when one is literally on one's own at sea. Our 1,200 mile voyage from Vancouver to San Diego was aptly named insofar as virtually everything aboard *Precious Metal* 'shook down' during a monumental five-day storm off the coast of Oregon. There's no question that we discovered *Precious Metal's* tenacity, together with the importance of teamwork and a capable, compatible crew.

Excitement was in the air as Jim, Guy, Joanne and I stowed away last-minute items in preparation for our 10.00am departure from the Royal Vancouver Yacht Club dock – for possibly the very last time. Our food and belongings were all stored in their specific places. *Precious Metal* was in perfect working order. Our spirits were high. The weather was a typical British Columbia stormy day which we all knew would be incidental in comparison to our expectations of offshore weather.

As a special final touch Royal Vancouver Yacht Club's Commodore Howard Bradbrooke and his lovely wife Lynn passed by us on their Saber 45 *Swift Current* proudly waving the Canadian flag and sending us their very best wishes. A small

*Precious Metal's shake-down crew (left to right): Guy Walters, Joanne Vickery,
Pamela Bendall and Jim Grace*

group of family members, partners and special friends gathered
on the dock in a torrential downpour.* Our 10.00am scheduled
departure was suddenly upon us and without further ado we said
our final good-byes and we were off!

The prestigious Royal Vancouver Yacht Club began to fade
into the distance along with Vancouver's extraordinary skyline of
high rises. All of my responsibilities in the yacht club and society
in general were now severed. After a lifetime of family, business
and community-minded dedication, it was a very strange feeling
to be completely free from societal responsibilities.

It took several days for my team to settle into a sailing mode
and understand *Precious Metal's* specific idiosyncrasies. Jim
established himself in the forward cabin, while Guy settled into
the bunk in the main salon. All of our bunks were secured with
lee cloths across the open sides to ensure no one inadvertently
rolled out of bed when the boat was heeled over. Joanne had the
luxury of sleeping in my aft stateroom since I generally slept in

---

* *Coincidentally, Howard and Lynn have subsequently sailed offshore and caught up to*
Precious Metal *in Panama City. In fact, I had the honour of line-handling aboard*
Swift Current *through the Panama Canal, as they continued on their voyage to the
Caribbean and further destinations.*

the cockpit on ocean crossings as a back-up to whoever is on watch. In fact, I have rarely settled into a deep sleep when sailing on the ocean insofar as my subconscious antennae are on guard for strange sounds, smells, bumps and flapping sails.

We stopped for one evening in Roche Harbour, Washington, to formally check out of Canada and into the United States. Another boat, *Eagle*, owned by my Canadian friend Barry Kerfoot, was also heading to California that same day. We radioed each other several times as our boats headed down Juan de Fuca Strait towards the open sea. That was the last time I heard from Barry for another six weeks! Barry had elected to harbour-hop along the United States coastline, while *Precious Metal* sailed 100 to 150 miles from the coast line theoretically to avoid off shore adverse current and weather conditions.

During an informal team meeting over dinner at Roche Harbour, we agreed that three-hour night watches for Jim, Guy and me were the most suitable and in adverse conditions we would double up as necessary. Joanne's responsibility as chef relieved her from doing night watches. With regards to alcohol consumption, my guideline aboard *Precious Metal* has always been one drink of choice after finishing a watch and a dinner hour cocktail or wine is acceptable in calm conditions – except for the person who has the first watch following dinner.

My reasoning was that sometimes after an exhausting watch, a short nip of alcohol allows for a much-needed sleep. I explained that during my two ocean races aboard boats that insisted on zero alcohol tolerance, I discovered that most of the crew had secretly brought their own mickey aboard and were surreptitiously sneaking small shots of their vices regardless of the rules. In fact, one of my funniest memories during one race was a virtual party every night in the forward sail locker sharing our tiny rations of alcohol, with one person on designated watch to advise us when the skipper's snoring ceased!

Jim's terrific Irish humour was a tremendous asset to the voyage, keeping us all in laughter throughout our journey. My first exposure to his candid humour was during our first night sail in the open ocean after rounding the notorious Cape Flattery. I was half-sleeping in the cockpit when Jim called me, "Pamela, I can hear the sound of an engine and I can see a light approaching from behind us, but I can't find any ships on the radar!" After inspecting the radar screen and the horizon I asked, "Are you sure you heard an engine?" He nodded affirmatively. "Well, I guess you should know that the crescent light that you see is the moon rising." I reported. We both had a small chuckle and as I was settling back into my sleeping bag he spoke again, "Pamela, one more thing before you go to sleep. When I'm on early morning watch, will the rising sun have an engine?"

Our first five days at sea were phenomenal. Joanne continued to surprise and delight us with three gourmet meals every day, while Guy and Jim spent many, albeit unsuccessful, hours patiently tending their fishing rods. The camaraderie aboard was terrific and we were making good progress under sail. My satellite phone was fully charged with ample minutes for at least a year and therefore I was able to phone Ilver each night with a position report and obtain our weather updates.

Early evening on our fifth day at sea (approximately 90 miles off the coast of Oregon) during my scheduled phone conversation with Ilver, he expressed concern about a serious weather system that was heading in our direction. Two massive high pressure systems were colliding straight in front of us with a small low pressure system developing underneath. I subsequently telephoned my trusted weather guru Greg Harms and asked his advice. Greg studied his available weather charts and became equally concerned.

He said we could expect 45- to 55-knot sustained winds from the north with sizable seas for the following five days. When I asked his advice as to whether we should head to port or weather the storm he replied, "Pamela, if it was me and my sailing buddies, we would welcome the storm and be fighting for the helm. It depends on the strength of your crew, which should be your determining factor. If your crew is weak or doubtful, you still have time to head to shore and wait out the storm in Coos Bay, Oregon."

I had a tough decision to make as skipper. Five days is a long time to endure an ocean storm. Conversely, heading to shore created two potential challenges: timing our entrance into Coos Bay with a pending storm approaching could potentially be dangerous insofar as the system could move faster than originally calculated; secondly, it would be at least a week for the storm and seas dissipate and *Precious Metal* could comfortably exit Coos Bay Harbour.

My crew had limited time scheduled for this voyage and would likely have to abandon me in Coos Bay to return home. Furthermore, I believed I had competent crew and this was an opportune time to discover *Precious Metal*'s true strengths and weaknesses at sea. My inclination was to weather the storm; however, I needed agreement amongst the entire crew before making my final decision.

After lengthy discussions highlighting all of the pros and cons, we collectively made a decision the following morning to brave the storm and maintain our course to San Diego. An ominous mood overshadowed our jovial state throughout the day as the skies ahead began to darken and the storm clouds began to form. What was I thinking? It was too late to alter course. We were committed to accepting whatever fury Mother Nature had in store for us. I could hear my late father's words of wisdom repeated over and over in my mind: "When the going gets tough, the tough get going."

As darkness set in, the seas began to build and build and build from behind us. We reefed (reduced) the main sail to the maximum setting and hoisted the inner stay sail (storm sail). Despite our virtual handkerchiefs for sails, our speed continued to increase as the storm's 50-knot winds began screaming through the rigging. Blackness surrounded the entire boat, blinding us from any visibility beyond the cockpit. The autopilot became overpowered, forcing us to hand-steer strictly by compass and instruments down the mountainous waves. It took tremendous concentration to stay on course as we surfed down each wave into cavernous dark troughs. At times, *Precious Metal* crested the swells with such force that it felt like the 50,000 pound beast was taking to the air!

Jim and I opted for the first watch, followed by Guy and Jim from midnight to 3.00am and Guy and me for the final sunrise stint. The intensity of concentration required to surf down the swells at the proper angle necessitated that we relieve each other every 30 minutes. Staying focused and on course was exhausting. We kept each other humoured and positive – becoming increasingly adept at steering as the evening unfolded.

Jim rarely imbibes any alcohol; yet, after finishing his intense watch at 3.00am he surfaced in the cockpit with an icy cold beer. Guy was at the helm and I sat across from Jim in the cockpit. Suddenly, a forceful wayward wave crashed into the starboard side of the hull and sent Jim flying over my head, through the vinyl screen window (breaking the snaps that secure the window) and landing on the deck just inside the lifeline. As he flew over my head my reflexes reacted and I instinctively grabbed onto him, slowing his flight. True to Jim's courageous character, he immediately regained his composure and climbed back into the cockpit brushing his shoulders saying, "I never knew I had wings!"

We didn't allow our minds think about the outcome of Jim's impromptu flight had I been sitting anywhere else and unable to slow his trajectory. At the time we were all wearing our safety harnesses in the cockpit, but only the standing helmsperson had their safety line secured to the boat. From this moment on, we tied ourselves onto the boat both inside and outside whenever possible – even when we were sleeping – to minimize any future inadvertent flights.

The following morning the next series of huge wayward waves simultaneously appeared from both sides of *Precious Metal*. Joanne had just finished tidying the galley after her best effort to serve us a breakfast of champions that consisted of assorted fruit, granola and tasty croissants. I often witnessed her managing in the galley straddled with her leg braced against the mast and the security belt around her waist as she dutifully kept our stomachs full and content. Suddenly, a wave hit the starboard hull so violently that our spare five-gallon water jug broke loose from its security straps and spilled the entire contents flooding my beautiful teak and holly floor. Fresh water began seeping through the cracks into the bilge as we desperately tried to mop up the mess.

Within seconds of our water spill another wave smashed against the port side of the boat and a huge crashing sound came from within the engine room. Using the strategically placed handrails that lead through the aft cabin and into the engine room, I found my way aft holding on with all of my strength and agility. Inside the engine room was a sight to behold. The three large drawers that contained my tools and spare parts had broken loose from their housings and the drawers with all of their contents spilled directly into the engine well (the space under the engine). To make matters worse, the water seeping from the galley had by then filled the engine well and my tools, light bulbs, electrical connectors, fuses and much more were floating around in the fresh water under the engine while the bilge pump was working full time to eliminate the water.

The balance of my day was spent crawling on my hands and knees, being tossed in every direction with a magnet to pick up metal objects and containers. Once everything was contained, my next challenge was to find a secure space aboard to stow away the drawers, given that their current locks were inadequate. Our only recourse was to store them on the aft bunk, meaning that Joanne and Riley had a new sleeping arrangement with three not-so-romantic tool drawers!

Guy won the prize for catching the first fish which he and Jim skillfully managed to bring aboard despite the angry seas. Once Jim had completed the task of filleting our sizable prize tuna, we stored several meals in containers keeping one in the fridge and placing the balance in the freezer. Jim and I were busy organizing our fish when the third and greatest wayward wave crashed into *Precious Metal* on our port side smothering the entire boat with sea water. Jim and I simultaneously flew across the galley and landed broadside against the dining table, breaking the table's base off the floor, landing underneath the table sitting against the far wall. As we regained our composure with the table top resting on our heads Jim was quick to remark, "Pamela, we have to stop meeting like this – people are going to talk!"

Understandably, Joanne's indoctrination to offshore sailing demanded far more courage than anyone had anticipated. It's far easier to cope in rough weather during the daytime when there's good visibility. The darkness of the night, together with the harrowing sounds and violent seas can be scary. Often during the night I would check on her in the aft cabin and find her and the tool drawers sliding every which way across the bunk. She admitted that her greatest reassurance at night was hearing us laugh aloud in the cockpit above her. As if to say, "It can't be that bad if they're all laughing."

As we progressed further south and into California waters, the temperature warmed allowing us to shed our heavy foul weather gear happily. By this time, none of us resembled a fashion statement. Simple tasks such as changing clothes are incredibly challenging in stormy conditions. Furthermore, it is a fruitless effort insofar as one cannot possibly stay groomed and clean during an ocean storm. We were constantly being soaked with sea water while being tossed and turned by the huge waves buffeting our boat. Ultimately we abandoned any semblance of decent grooming.

Our futile efforts of having daily sponge baths were our only attempts at hygiene; hence, all of our 'storm' clothes went directly into a pile destined for the garbage bin. Jim wrote me a humorous letter three weeks after he arrived back in Canada saying, "I still ask my wife to hold my coffee cup when I use the bathroom in the morning!"

Poor Riley gained more and more sympathy with each passing day because he refused to venture on the forward deck to do his business during the storm. Prior to departing Canada, I had invested extensive time and money into every imaginable strategy of doggie bathroom aboard, which he refused to use

This is how Riley looked after 63.5 hours at sea without being able to do his business

and simply opted to venture onto the foredeck – usually when no one was looking. During the storm, Joanne and I repeatedly suited him up in his life jacket and leash and used every form of encouragement and bribe to get him to venture on deck but he dug in his paws and refused our enticements. His adorable huge brown eyes seemed to bulge further and further out of his head with each passing day. Finally, after 68 hours of containment Riley acquiesced and sprinted to the bow with a sense of urgency. We all cheered with relief as he pranced back to the cockpit with an apparent skip in his gate and possibly a smile on his cute little face. Relief at last.

On our fifth and final day of the storm we began to notice a lot of freighter and ship traffic heading to and from the Los Angeles region. On one occasion we were on a collision course with a freighter and I radioed the captain on the VHF advising him that I was altering course. He politely responded that he would go around me saying, "I can see that you're under sail in a big storm so it's a lot easier for me to change course." Once the ship had safely passed us he called again and advised me that *Precious Metal* was barely visible on his radar. I was surprised because a the steel hull usually reflects a strong radar signal. He said that the swells were so large and the troughs were so deep that the only time *Precious Metal* showed a blip on the radar screen was when she momentarily crested a wave.

He also mentioned that he was surprised to find such a tiny boat weathering such a huge storm. Our fortitude was reinforced again several days after our arrival into San Diego when we learned that a famous sailor and racer was 50 miles from *Precious Metal* at the height of the storm when he hailed a ship to rescue him and chose to scuttle his boat!

Calmness finally prevailed as we approached California's Catalina Islands. The silence and stillness of the ocean was captivating as the swells abated bringing sunshine and clear skies. How could the ocean be so incredibly wild one day and so passive the next? We stopped briefly in the Catalina Islands for fuel and did our final overnight passage to San Diego, arriving at sunrise the following morning. Witnessing San Diego's cityscape with the brilliant sun accenting the tall buildings as we approached the harbour entrance brought a sense of exhilaration to my soul that is rarely experienced. We had made it!

Despite feeling the sense of being in a washing machine for five solid days and nights, *Precious Metal* resembled the exact opposite of 'clean and tidy' as she humbly approached the prestigious San Diego Yacht Club Marina – which became my luxurious home for the next six weeks. My crew and I were treated like royalty when we arrived and for the following few days we celebrated our epic voyage in style.

All good things eventually come to an end and soon Guy, Jim and Joanne departed *Precious Metal* leaving Riley and me with a broken-down boat that took six long weeks of arduous work to repair. What was I thinking? It never occurred to me until then that boat maintenance and repairs are a fact of life for cruisers. Cruising life is often referred to as "Fixing your boat in exotic places." My deadline to have *Precious Metal* seaworthy was October 27 when she was registered to enter the Baja HaHa Regatta from San Diego to Cabo San Lucas, Mexico.

The Baja HaHa was a fun, annual cruisers' event hosted by California's most reputable sailing magazine, *Latitude 38*. Over 150 cruising boats participated in this week-long event. The Grand Phoobah, Richard Spindler, and his capable partner Dona hosted a number of associated activities throughout the event including beach parties, daily radio check-ins and entertaining galas at the start and finish. In its 15th year (in 2008), one of the greatest features of the HaHa was the opportunity to meet fellow cruisers who were also exploring Mexico and establish meaningful, long-time friendships.

My wonderful friends Noel and Jennifer Villard joined *Precious Metal* for the 2008 HaHa together with another friend, Murray Ball, and Ilver. Our participation in the event was somewhat limited due to a burst hose line and pump in the forward head that required a fast run to Cabo San Lucas for repairs. Nonetheless, we thoroughly enjoyed the festivities that were available to us.

CHAPTER 8

Mexico – A Cruiser's Paradise

2008 - 2010

Documenting all of my momentous experiences during *Precious Metal*'s three seasons in Mexico would take a lifetime.* Suffice to say that, Mexico offers the very best cruising lifestyle of all the destinations I've explored. It's stunningly beautiful, has excellent cruiser-friendly facilities and amenities, the weather is almost perfect every single day, it's affordable, has a rich and fascinating culture, the cruising community is terrific and the local Mexican people are absolutely delightful.

My first priority upon my arrival in Mexico was to address my apparent lack of mechanical, electrical and general maintenance knowledge aboard *Precious Metal*. I needed to face the harsh reality that it was time to get my hands dirty and begin handling my own maintenance and repairs. I began by developing a business plan that incorporated every device, part and machinery dealing with all aspects of the boat's functionality: what it is, what is does, how to fix it, the necessary spare parts and the tools required to

* *For the purposes of this book, I have combined all three seasons of my time in Mexico into one chapter. In fact, after Sail Fest in season two, I departed for the Galapagos Islands, Peru and many more destinations that are highlighted in the following chapters. I returned to Mexico one year later to continue my efforts as chairperson of Sail Fest, which was when the tsunami from Japan took place.*

maintain and repair it. Unquestionably, the greatest number of 'what was I thinking' moments on this entire five-year voyage have related to maintenance and repairs of my 50,000 pound sailing vessel in distant, remote, often solo situations.

Truthfully, when I departed Canada I thought I was pretty competent with the workings of my boat. I just didn't know what I didn't know. Certainly, I knew how to change my filters, alternator belts, oil and simple tasks; but I had no comprehension of the magnitude of work that's required to maintain every system on my boat. I hate to stereotype; however, few women are raised and socialized in the field of mechanics, tools, electronics, filter systems, battery systems and so on. One has to be prepared to get dirty and spend time in precarious positions aboard the boat that simply aren't lady-like. That said, it has always been incredibly gratifying to take apart a mechanical or electrical boat system successfuly, maintain or repair it and assemble it all back together. Furthermore, boat systems are generally quite simple and make a lot of sense. Although initially daunting and definitely filthy, anyone can learn boat maintenance.

My maintenance regime was never finished. Listed are some of my ongoing chores to illustrate exactly how much work this exotic life entails:

- engine maintenance
- fuel system maintenance:
- 11 filter systems
- two alternators with belts,
- batteries
- cables
- oil changes
- maintaining nine pumps
- electrical connectors throughout the boat
- bilge cleaning
- continual rust work (rust never sleeps!)
- wood maintenance
- deck work
- canvas work

- rigging maintenance
- sail maintenance
- dinghy and outboard maintenance
- water-maker maintenance
- gas generator maintenance
- hose clamps throughout the entire boat
- mould cleaning and prevention
- stanchions and lifelines
- safety equipment
- anchor chain
- boat bottom
- sheets and lines
- head maintenance
- general cleaning and polishing

Aside from the gratification from conquering the art of successfully completing a maintenance project, there are a number of very good reasons why every boater should be competent in boat maintenance and repairs. I learned that if a part or system has not been maintained properly, it will break down and will need to be repaired. Furthermore, I have discovered that if I have not maintained it, I won't likely know how to repair it; nor will I have the spare parts and available tools. Maintenance can be done at one's leisure; however, a repair will invariably be required at an inopportune time, under duress and could potentially occur in a dangerous situation. Importantly, knowledge is power. The more I have understood my boat, the more independent I have become, which ultimately has resulted in a higher level of fulfilment and enjoyment.*

The fear of cruising through Mexico, often alone, dominated the minds of my family and friends in Canada. So much so that even I thought that I should be scared. Ilver had planned to join me at various intervals between his work commitments, but we also knew that I would be spending much of my time in solitude. A wonderful man named Sergio in La Paz specialized

A detailed document entitled Introductory Step by Step Boat Maintenance for Women from a Woman's Perspective is Appendix II in the back of this book.

in fabricating stainless steel at a reasonable price. I hired Sergio to construct custom safety bars to fit on my hatches and companionway (main doorway) to allow the circulation of air at night when I locked myself inside the boat. Sergio dutifully performed this task saying, "Pamela, I take this job seriously – to keep the bad men out and the good men in!"

What was I thinking? Tragically, the media has given Mexico and many impoverished regions in Central and South America an unjustifiably negative reputation for crime – as though there are no thefts or homicides in the United States or Canada. Rare incidents involving theft have occurred on several cruising boats during my voyage, although they were few and far between. I have never experienced an incident that has threatened my personal safety. In fact, I have never used Sergio's safety bars, nor do I lock myself inside the boat at night. If anything, on most nights I have generally slept in the open cockpit under the stars!

My four personal rules of conduct have always been quite basic and easy to follow:

- Always be respectful – the citizens of these countries have their own way of taking the law into their hands
- Always return to the boat at a reasonable hour after dark – most incidents are alcohol and drug related and take place during the night
- Never flaunt money, wealth or jewellery – it's an invitation to these impoverished people; always lock the boat when leaving – they will be watching
- Never leave the boat when tradespeople are aboard; and never entertain any invitations to buy drugs from street vendors

As a special note, I will always remember my friend Jennifer Villard's very savvy late mother Jane Adams who lived a full and active life until her passing at 86. Jane shared two exemplary quotes that have always made me smile and will live with me forever: "Nothing good happens after midnight," and, "Always leave the party while they're still enjoying your company." Both of these mottos hold a lot of credence, particularly in foreign countries and originate from a very special woman.

I did experience one fairly serious incident involving the Mexican drug trade that occurred during my first year in Mexico on a night passage between Manzanillo and the tiny anchorage of Maruata, 80 miles to the south. The passage is too long to complete in the daytime, so it's customary to depart Manzanillo around 4.00pm in the afternoon, timing the arrival for anchorage at sunrise the following day.

Ilver was aboard and we were buddy boating with a couple named Dave and Helen aboard their boat *Jammin*. At approximately midnight, while Ilver was sleeping soundly, I sailed within six feet of a floating black Styrofoam rectangular box that was roughly six feet long by two feet deep. At first, I didn't think too much about it, other than it was a hazard to *Jammin* who was sailing less than a mile behind us. I promptly radioed them by VHF to warn of this navigation hazard.

What was I thinking? In my naivety, it never occurred to me that we were in the path of a horrendous drug bust! Suddenly, a fairly sizeable boat appeared on my radar screen from out of nowhere approximately one mile off my starboard beam. It paralleled my course by exactly one mile for a substantial amount of time – enough time for the suspicious object to drift behind me. The boat had no lights and was not visible with my binoculars.

Strangely, the mystery boat slipped behind me and immediately stood a mile off *Jammin*'s starboard beam. All of this activity was detected on my radar. Again, I radioed *Jammin* to notify them about the mystery boat. Eventually, my radar indicated that the mystery boat had slipped behind *Jammin* for about 10 minutes (presumably in proximity to the floating object) and then vanished off the radar screen. Shortly thereafter, I detected another radar sighting five miles ahead of me, again with no lights. This boat maintained a five-mile distance ahead of *Precious Metal* for the balance of the night. It wouldn't answer any radio call. Needless to say, this proved to be a very prolonged and nerve-wracking six-hour period of darkness. What were these suspicious boats doing navigating the waters at night with no lights or radio contact? I collected my two canisters of bear spray, together with a few flare guns and anxiously scanned the horizon counting the minutes until sunrise.

The VHF radio shocked me into attention as I was veering towards the anchorage at sunrise. "Sailboat approaching Maruata, this is the Mexican Navy. Please identify yourself." I politely answered his broken English questions in my broken Spanish.

"Be prepared. We are coming to board your boat!"

This sounded incredibly serious. They subsequently radioed *Jammin* with equally direct sternness. Instantly, three small open-air Navy *pangas* (typical Mexican fishing boat) dashed across the five-mile stretch from the large vessel that had stood ahead of us all night. Aha! It had been the Mexican Navy monitoring our position five miles ahead of us all night.

Each of the three boats had three (very!) young uniformed Mexicans holding their automatic rifles as though we were under attack. One boat approached *Precious Metal*, a second went to *Jammin*, while the third remained equidistant between our boats. Their serious looks indicated that they meant business. They were on a mission.

As they climbed aboard, one man went directly to the stern of *Precious Metal* and stood at attention with his rifle by his side. The second man stayed dutifully at the open gate, also at attention with his rifle. Finally, the man with seniority shook my hand and introduced himself as Mañuel before proceeding to ask the questions on his clipboard. Things didn't quite unfold as professionally as he'd hoped when he discovered that his pen had no ink and I think he felt a little silly. I graciously provided him with a pen and proceeded to carry on with the questioning.

When asked, I told him my name, Pamela. "Ah, Pamela Anderson!" he replied with his eyes desperately hopeful. The other two boys standing guard began to giggle and could no longer contain their serious composure. "No," I confessed. "My name is Pamela Bendall, but Pamela Anderson is also Canadian." This was enough to ingratiate us with our Navy contingent and from then onwards the conversation became much more jovial.

They never searched *Precious Metal* and they were pleased to accept some cold soft drinks.

Once the interrogation was completed, he began to address the real reason why they were aboard. In fact, the floating object that I skirted the previous evening was a drug drop which was under surveillance. They were waiting for it to be picked up by the drug runners when our boats sailed past. He believed that the mission was abandoned, when the mystery boat took off into darkness. Mañuel also seemed genuinely relieved that we hadn't stopped to inquire about the package. Undoubtedly, the story would have had a much graver ending. "Please don't sail your boat at night in these waters. It's very safe during the day time but not at night."

Once Mañuel was satisfied that he had made his point, he asked me if we needed anything? "In fact, my water-maker isn't functioning properly," I said. "We're getting a little low on water, although my buddy intends to give us some." With this, Mañuel instructed his subordinate to radio to the mother ship to prepare three five-gallon jugs of water and bring them to *Precious Metal.*

The scene was incredibly sweet when the fourth Navy *panga* arrived with our water. Aboard the craft and in full uniform was the Navy captain himself. He was graciously respectful and polite when he boarded our boat. Then, after introducing himself and the customary handshakes, he said, "From one captain to another, I have come to give you a weather report." I thanked him profusely. The scene was absolutely amazing and had a very happy ending.

During this first season in Mexico, Ilver was able to devote enough time away from work to allow us to sail together as far south as Zihuatanejo. Ironically, both Ilver and I had independently visited (in previous relationships) this charming seaside fishing village 15 years earlier, before it became a popular tourist destination. As if it was yesterday, I remember sitting on the beach outside my hotel looking at all of the sailboats anchored in the bay and saying to myself, "Someday I want to be anchored in this bay on my own sailboat." My dream had finally come true.

On one of our first evenings ashore we were dining at a lovely

Mexican Navy officers and Pamela aboard Precious Metal

restaurant and a young, adorable little Mexican boy approached me with his big brown eyes asking me to buy some of his candies for five cents apiece. I complied and asked him, "What are you doing up so late? Shouldn't you be home in bed getting ready for school tomorrow?" I doubt that he understood me because these children speak in an Indian dialect. My friend sitting across the table said, "Pamela, the kids that beg here at night are incredibly poor. This little boy probably doesn't have a home, nor is he able to go to school."

What was I thinking? My heart sank. I was speechless. He explained that these children who are begging come from squatters' communities outside of town. They are loaded into pick-up trucks in the late afternoon and deposited on the beach under the supervision of a parent or adult who is never far away. It's the only life that they know.

Fortunately, the following week, I was able to make amends and compensate for my insensitive remark at a truly meaningful local event called Sail Fest.

The cruising community hosts a radio network in the mornings in every sizeable anchorage throughout Mexico where we all check in, find out what's going on in town, discover where to find what we need and there's usually a weather report. During our first week in Zihuatanejo we were told on the morning Net that an annual Sail Fest event was taking place the following week and they needed volunteers from the cruising community to assist in coordinating the sailing events. We learned that Sail Fest is a major fund-raising project that provides new schools for local impoverished children. Given my blunder in the restaurant several nights earlier, I was delighted to commit to attending the upcoming meeting.

Only a handful of cruisers showed up for the meeting and suddenly I found myself in the position of co-chairperson – along with a man named Bill from the sailing vessel *Some Day*. We had less than a week to learn about and coordinate two sailing events. Until the previous day I had never heard of Sail Fest! I became incredibly passionate about this project and ultimately chaired the cruising activities for a subsequent five years.

Now in its 13th year, Sail Fest has built eight schools with over 50 classrooms and has educated over 5,000 of Mexico's poorest children who would otherwise never see the inside of a classroom. During Sail Fest week, locals and visitors in the community participate in both land-based and sailing activities that raise in the range of $40,000 to $80,000. This money provides the capital to build the schools and cover the operating costs. Each school is built and maintained by local male villagers. The women of the community prepare a hearty daily meal for the students, which is also funded by Sail Fest activities. The Sail Fest website (www.sailfest.org) has a complete description of the event and also links to the parent organization, *Por Los Niños* (www.porlosninos.com) which oversees the construction of the schools and management of the funds.

I still get shivers down my back when I think about Oliver, an extremely bright and engaging young man, who was one of our first students in the program. Last year Oliver was awarded a $48,000.00 scholarship to a United States multicultural university! This is a heart-warming testimony to the success of the event and the tremendous impact that Sail Fest has on the small Mexican town of Zihuatanejo and its surrounding villages.

Needless to say, both Bill and I were incredibly busy during our first endeavour as organizers of the sailing events. We also had a lot of fun. Cruising boats began to arrive in the bay just in time for the start of our first event: the Sail Fest Parade. The cruising vessels host locals and visitors aboard their boats for a $30.00 per person contribution, who enjoy a two-hour ride around both Zihuatanejo and Ixtapa bays. The final phase of the parade passes by the port captain's boat and each of the guests salutes the Captain and douses their flag. Then the boats are free to continue sailing or enjoy the many aspects of Zihuatanejo and surrounding bays for the balance of the afternoon. Warm smiles always appear on the guests' faces as they disembark from their respective host boats.

The second sailing event is a pursuit race that begins in Zihuatanejo Bay and circles a small island two miles out of the harbour. Again, guests are invited to race on the boats for a $30.00 per person contribution. Given that there's seasonally minimal wind and most of the cruising boats aren't suited for racing, it's a fun event and never taken too seriously. People can place bets on their own boat or competing boats and half of the money raised goes into the Sail Fest kitty. Fun prizes are awarded for both events at the final Sail Fest ceremony.

Land-based activities – such as live concerts with tremendous local talent, a chilli cook-off, kids' beach day (and much more) – take place during the week. One of my favourite events is the day that we tour the schools that have been built with Sail Fest funding. There's rarely a dry eye in the group as we explore the schools and witness these darling young children who are proudly dressed in their uniforms (they otherwise would not have clothes or shoes) and keenly attentive to their teacher. I'm confident these children don't have to be coerced into getting out of bed and going to school. For these young children, going to school is an incredible privilege given their impoverished lifestyle and the horrific conditions that they previously endured.

Beyond the tremendous satisfaction that comes with

One of Zihuatanejo's seven schools built with Sail Fest revenue

doing my small part to leave a modest legacy in this wonderful community, I personally benefited from Sail Fest due to the wonderful and enduring friendships that were made when people joined together to create a meaningful project. So many fellow boaters gave their all in terms of time and expertise to make Sail Fest week a success which was truly gratifying. My wonderful late father Gordon Roy always preached, "Try to leave everywhere you go a better place because you were there." Sail Fest's hundreds of volunteers, both land-based and sailors, should feel proud of their dedication towards making Zihuatanejo a much better place.

Generally, the weather in Mexico is balmy and dry during the cruising season between November and May. That said, I've experienced one hurricane, one weather spout, one earthquake and two tsunamis.*

Hurricane Rick tormented Mazatlan at the beginning of my second season in Mexico. My long-time friend from the investment business, Bruce Schwenger, was visiting me in

---

* My experience during a volcano took place while sailing in Japan in 1989 and is described in Appendix I of this book.

anticipation of doing an overnight sail with me to La Paz, on the Baja Peninsula. As Rick veered towards Mazatlan's coast with raging 70-mile-an-hour winds, every boat owner in the marina was scrambling to secure their vessels and everything on board safely in anticipation of the approaching storm.

Bruce and I, along with several other cruisers, rented a condominium that overlooked the harbour and watched our boats throughout the 24-hour blow. *Precious Metal* rocked and rolled wildly but survived unscathed. A few boats and docks suffered minimal damage; however, the local buildings that weren't well built experienced considerable damage. Unsecured tiles from the roof tops were flying through the air like missiles, smashing windows and cars. An entire palm tree was uprooted and literally flew through the wall of one condominium building! Sadly, Hurricane Rick consumed all of Bruce's holiday time and he had to return home having never left the dock. This was the third time he had visited *Precious Metal* when an incident occurred prohibiting us from sailing and consequently he was beginning to doubt that *Precious Metal* even had any sails.

The earthquake occurred while I was in Zihuatanejo, although the epicentre (7.0 on the Richter Scale) originated in Mexico City hundreds of miles away. I was anchored in the bay contently drinking my morning coffee and concentrating on my computer when suddenly, I heard a huge thunderous rumbling sound right outside the boat. It sounded like a giant freighter engine starting right beside my boat – but I knew that freighters never entered that bay. The seas surrounding *Precious Metal* began to ripple. Curious, I looked outside and walked around the decks, but found nothing that could have created this startling occurrence.

Just when I began to think that I was imagining things, another cruiser called on the radio and stated, "I'm not sure if I'm going crazy, but did anyone else experience something really odd a few minutes ago, like a giant imaginary thunderbolt?" We all raced to our radios and thanked the fellow for coming forward with his admission. The earthquake in Mexico City was confirmed shortly thereafter. I always wondered if earthquakes can be felt on the ocean and now I know!

The quaint Mexican community of La Cruz, on the outskirts of Puerto Vallarta, was the home of the weather spout. I was sleeping soundly in the marina and was awakened to my friend Barry's panicking voice on the VHF in the middle of the night. "Pamela, *Precious Metal*. This is the *Eagle*. Are you awake?" It took me a few seconds to gather my senses. Then, I rushed into my cockpit and answered him. "Now I am," I said. "What's happening?" Barry was anchored in the bay outside the marina and a huge storm that hadn't been predicted suddenly blew up causing violent winds and huge swells. My clock read 5.00am. "There's a big storm happening out here and my anchor is dragging my boat towards shore. I need help getting my anchor up. Please come immediately." The *Eagle* was a 52-foot older and heavier traditional boat, therefore not easily manoeuvrable by one person in stormy conditions.

I immediately jumped into my dinghy and raced towards the marina channel exit that is lined with two breakwaters constructed with piles of huge boulders. Sure enough, a raging storm was howling as I exited the protected marina. Barry's boat could barely be seen through the darkness and sea spray, but I could tell that he was in trouble. The *Eagle* was behaving like a bucking bronco. Suddenly, to my horror, my dinghy motor stopped. The tumultuous seas and relentless winds were instantly pushing me towards the breakwater where the breaking waves were crashing against the rocks. I was in trouble. Big trouble.

To make matters worse, in my haste to assist Barry, I neglected to put on my life vest and my dinghy paddles were on the dock because I had been varnishing them the previous day. No radio, no life vest, no paddles and no engine in a raging storm and complete darkness. What was I thinking? I screamed for help but the howling winds silenced my calls. Why did my engine fail? My heart was pounding. I had to stay calm and act quickly. Hastily, I reached down to my propeller and discovered fishing net wrapped tightly around it. I scrambled to release the netting and managed to free it and start the motor within seconds of being smashed against the rocks. Once I was clear of the rocks I was able to calm myself, knowing that I nearly needed to be rescued from doing a rescue!

My next challenge was to find a way to board Barry's boat safely in the crashing waves. As my dinghy came alongside Barry's hull, I waited for a wave to lift me within close proximity of *Eagle*'s deck and succeeded in climbing aboard. I immediately took over the helm while Barry attended to bringing up his anchor. Normally, it's easy to steer into the wind but the gusts were so powerful I used my entire strength to control the steering. Finally, after a lot of aggravation, *Eagle*'s anchor was on deck and we motored into the marina. Barry's boat was safe. I was safe but exhausted. It was time for me to go back to bed and try to get some sleep.

No sooner was my head on the pillow when another voice yelled on the radio, "Prepare your boats for hurricane conditions! There's a massive weather spout crossing the bay and heading in our direction." By this time the sun was rising and a giant dark tornado was coming across Banderas Bay directly towards us. I frantically scrambled onto the dock to collect *Precious Metal*'s belongings that I had been working on – including the paddles. Once everything on board the boat was secure, I was able to witness the weather spout's approach. It was an incredibly dramatic sight. Just before it reached the marina it waned and dissipated – before our eyes. With so much excitement for one early morning I decided not to return to bed again for fear of another radio call announcing yet another catastrophe.

I was in Acapulco for the first of my two tsunamis. Little Riley and I were enjoying our morning walk around 8.00am when a friend phoned me with the news of an earthquake that had occurred overnight in Chile. The associated tsunami was scheduled to arrive into the Acapulco region by 11.00am. This gave me three hours to get out of the crowded bay and into deep water. Two other cruising boats were anchored nearby. I radioed to both of them and suggested we all depart as quickly as possible. One of the boats agreed wholeheartedly and immediately prepared their boat for departure. The second boat was manned by an elderly couple and they sounded more hesitant. Eventually, after I prompted them further, the skipper admitted that, "My wife has a hair appointment at 2.00pm which she doesn't want to miss." What were they thinking? The elderly couple eventually agreed to forego the hair appointment and followed us out to sea where no effects of the tsunami were felt and little damage occurred along the Mexican coastline.

The second tsunami was a much bigger event and was influenced by Japan's horrific earthquake in March 2011. I was anchored in Zihuatanejo during my third cruising season when news of Japan's overnight earthquake was announced on our morning Net. Calculations based on the speed of a tsunami wave crossing the Pacific Ocean brought the potential tsunami into our region between approximately 12.00noon and 1.00pm local time. Each boat in the anchorage had time to decide whether to head out to sea and away from land hazards, or snug down the anchor and hope for the best.

I was looking forward to this day because I had the privilege of being invited to lunch by a local Mexican family who owned my favourite restaurant on Las Gatos Beach, directly across the bay from the anchorage. Noyo and his entire family had become wonderful friends and Noyo was invaluable in terms of assisting me with Sail Fest activities. As an added feature, Noyo's elderly mother had agreed to provide me with her secret fish ceviche recipe which was to die for. We were all so excited about this luncheon and family get-together, which had been planned for several weeks.

Upon notice of the tsunami, an evacuation order was placed on all Zihuatanejo beaches and the local fisherman hastily worked towards clearing their *pangas* from the entire surrounding area. Sadly, I radioed Noyo early in the morning and advised him that we had to postpone our lunch.

At approximately noon, two mountainous waves swept through the bay simultaneously, followed by a normal wave pattern. In typical fashion, the cruising community had a small discussion on the VHF and concurred that these waves were the extent of the tsunami. Everyone seemed satisfied that it was a non-event. This was a relief knowing that I could probably resurrect our lunch date. I radioed to Noyo who assured me that his family were delighted and looked forward to our visit. I jumped in the dinghy and motored across the one-mile stretch of water to Noyo's family restaurant.

Needless to say, the beach was deserted. One plastic table with a Mexican-style table cloth was perched on the beach in front of Noyo's family's restaurant surrounded by several white plastic chairs. We brought my dinghy to the high water mark on the beach and secured it by digging its anchor into the sand. After our initial greetings and pleasantries, I was ushered to our table and Noyo's mom graciously began to prepare her legendary ceviche.

Captivated by her detailed explanation and demonstration on making ceviche, I wasn't paying attention to the shoreline. When I finally looked aside several minutes into my cooking class, the dinghy was floating and water was rapidly engulfing the entire beach right up to my knees! I raced to capture the dinghy from floating away and suddenly the enormous tide flushed out to sea. The beach in front was the length of a football field. We brought our table, chairs and dinghy to high ground and then stood mesmerized by the incredible force of the tsunami. The extent and speed of the powerful ocean surges was daunting. It was spellbinding.

Suddenly, from out of nowhere, at least a dozen excited children came running onto the beach – all carrying their floating swimming toys (boogie boards, life rings, inflatable toys, etc) and went dashing into the ocean.

As the ocean emptied out of the bay, the children were gone! They vanished from our sight and were last seen heading out to sea riding their various inflatable toys and boogie boards. I was aghast! I screamed, "The children are gone!" No sooner had I called out in desperation, did the children come back into sight on a reverse surge riding the next wave into the bay. They zoomed by our beach and into the opposite bay at an incredible velocity, their cheers of joy and laughter infectious. They happily waved to their parents and families who stood on the beach and eagerly waved back to them!

Even more incredible was that these surging waves continued for the better part of the afternoon and the kids innocently continued to indulge feverishly in their ultimate playground. They attached themselves to mooring buoys and water skied in the raging water. Many of the parents rushed to grab their cameras and began taking photos and videos of their children. I was astonished by the blatant lack of fear displayed by the children, parents and entire community.

Needless to say, our cooking class was abandoned for another day, as I needed to return to *Precious Metal* as quickly as possible. I was confident that her anchor was securely set, although these circumstances were extreme enough to warrant concern. On the next incoming surge a host of villagers helped to launch the dinghy quickly and I was literally pulled out of the beach area on an outgoing wave.

Precious Metal was fine, although a number of other boats were scrambling to secure their anchors and one boat was beached. My knot meter indicated that *Precious Metal* was often moving nearly one knot per hour on her anchor with each surging wave! Surprisingly, these tsunami surges lasted into the early evening. According to Noyo, all of the children returned to their homes safely after an exciting and invigorating afternoon.

One additional special highlight that has occurred during my lengthy stays in Zihuatanejo is that my friend Nick Glen and his wife Anne, along with several family members, plan their annual tropical winter holiday in a local resort at the same time. Nick and I had a long history of working together in the investment business and have always maintained a terrific friendship. In fact, they hosted my retirement party from the business in 2001 at their prestigious home in Vancouver.

Our conversations have often delved into the topic of retirement and the 'appropriate' time to exit our careers. Before my retirement, Nick and I shared similar successful business models. He has continued to work hard and his business has grown substantially over the years. My alternate path of early retirement has provided me with some of the best and most interesting years of my life, although my nest egg isn't remotely close to his.

The question of when to retire has always been a bit of a lottery. My cherished late father Gordon Roy devoted the majority of his life towards a successful career in the investment industry and suffered a major stroke when he was 76, three years after his retirement, rendering him paralysed and unable to speak in his final years. He never had an opportunity to pursue his dreams. I suspect that he worked so hard his entire life that he never had time to develop any dreams beyond his career.

Conversely one could end up like Frank in Yalapa, Mexico – who presumably misjudged the timing of his retirement. A fund-raising bulletin was posted on the local coffee shop wall requesting that "People rally on Friday night to help Frank." I asked the waitress what happened to Frank (my mind raced between major accident, child's illness, medical travesty, house fire...?) "Oh, he ran out of money. Just spent more than he had," she said nonchalantly. It's always been comforting to know that if I run out of money I can always go to Yalapa and be the beneficiary of a local fund-raiser!

My recommendation to Nick and others who have been contemplating retirement has been two-fold: Don't wait until you're too old physically and mentally to be able to follow your dreams and passions; and, always leave your business on a 'high'. (Leave the party while they're still enjoying your company.) My decision to take early retirement satisfied both of these criteria. I would not have done it any other way.

What Am I Thinking?

Witnessing the mind blowing experience with the Zihuatanejo children during the tsunami cast a new light on my interpretation of fear and the contrasts between the cultures of (so-called) developed and developing countries. Why would these people be afraid? They don't have televisions, smart phones and the media bombarding them every day with reasons to be afraid. They aren't inundated with rules and regulations that restrict their confidence, independence and curiosity. There are no lawyers in these communities to threaten litigation.

The children are completely comfortable with their natural environment. They're not over-protected. These children have been raised learning survival skills since their infancy, as I've witnessed in all of the Third World cultures that I've explored. Naturally, I would not endorse that our children ride tsunami waves or embrace Third World lifestyles. Nevertheless, there's a lot to be said for many aspects of these cultures.

Imagine the life of these children who live with no fear – at least the fear that we know in our society. They're confident enough to play in tidal waves and their parents are simply on hand to share in their joy and take photographs. Every morning, after presumably some kind of food, they find their way to school. Some walk long distances, take buses and others paddle across strong currents along the rivers and estuaries in a home-made dugout canoe. They safely get to school and home again, often in adverse conditions, without anyone chaperoning them or signing them in and out.

After school these children play wholeheartedly outside until dark: on the beach, in the water, in the parks and the local school ground or soccer field. Their toys are made from natural materials that they find in their local environment. No one locks their doors (if they have doors on their homes), there's little or no crime in these harmonious communities and the people always seem happy and cheerful. Sundays are a huge celebration when the entire family and extended family get together for an elaborate feast on the beach, in the park or at their homes. It's likely the term 'bullying' is not in their vocabulary.

Fear seems to have surreptitiously crept into our western society since my childhood; coincidentally with the advent of the television. My family and schoolmates walked several miles to and from school in blistering Montreal snowstorms (yes, uphill both ways!) and never considered being driven or chaperoned. It was a built-in fitness regimen, as well as an opportunity to develop meaningful friendships with the local children who lived on the same route. Some of my childhood romances developed on the route to school, or perhaps a short detour away.

We always played outside until dark and never considered watching our (one!) television – except for a few hours on the weekends. After all, we only had 12 channels. We rode our bicycles everywhere and our parents often had no idea about our whereabouts. It wasn't that they didn't care or love us; people weren't afraid in those days.

Virtually every aspect of our society has safety standards and regulations that are becoming more and more onerous due to fear. One would think that the increasing number of rules and restrictions that we place on our society would tend to eliminate fear, but instead I believe that they intensify paranoia. What are we teaching our children when we impose more and more rules and restrictions in their lives to 'protect' them? How will they ever cope with adversity in life if they've never been exposed to it? How will they gain confidence and think for themselves if they're stifled by fear?

This is not to say that we should ignore crime completely, or never lock our doors. Yes, gangs and pathological criminals exist in every corner of the world and we always need to remain vigilant. We are exposed every day by the media to horrific crimes and catastrophes ('happy' stories don't sell newspapers) that can easily perpetuate fear in our minds; however, the media fail to mention that the majority of the seven billion people in the world enjoyed a safe and harm-free day.

I have travelled extensively in over 100 countries globally, many twice, often alone and crossing all social-economic boundaries. Never has my personal safety been challenged. My only theft to report was 30 years ago. Ironically, my former husband Michael and our two young boys (ages six months and six years at the time) had been travelling through many distant corners of Africa for three months. The day after I returned to

Whitehorse, Yukon (Canada) my purse was taken out my car in front of my son's day care centre.

Crime can happen anywhere in the world. I believe that 99.9 percent of the people on this planet are truly wonderful, caring and essentially honest individuals. We're all simply trying to get through our precious lives in the very best way with what we have been given.

CHAPTER 9

Mexico to the Galapagos Islands and Peru: A Dream Come True

March 15, 2010

ALL MY HOPES and dreams of an epic offshore sailing voyage were answered during the 25-day ocean passage from Huatulco, Mexico, to Lima, Peru, via the Galapagos Islands. My crew, Jim and Doug, were terrific which contributed to an exceedingly harmonious camaraderie aboard. *Precious Metal* was on her best behaviour (for the most part), the weather cooperated as well as could be expected and the respective region of the ocean displayed an abundance of marine life and sea birds.

What was I thinking when I decided to abandon my wonderful sailing friends and glorious cruising lifestyle I so dearly enjoyed in Mexico to head out on a non-traditional sailing route to the Galapagos Islands and then Peru? Most savvy sailors would say that I was "going the wrong way."

My lifelong dream since Miss Patterson's (Oak Ridge School, Montreal, Quebec) Grade Three geography project had been to explore Peru because of its rich culture and renowned physical highlights such as the Amazon River, Amazon Rainforest and Andes Mountains. Peru's fascinating ancient Inca civilization of Macchu Pichu was just opening as a tourist destination when I was a little girl putting my geography project together.

The Galapagos Islands entered my wish list after reading Charles Darwin's book *The Origin of Species* in the early 1980s.

Consequently, my visions the Galapagos Islands were of rare giant 500-pound tortoises and unique marine iguanas, penguins and other species introduced via the Humbolt Current and freely living their natural existence on these unique Ecuadorian islands.

I researched the multitude of sailing guides to these countries and discovered to my frustration that the traditional routes to these chosen destinations were not only lengthy from Mexico but were also cumbersome in terms of the necessary protocol used in entering, exiting and staying in each respective country. Ecuador seemed to be changing their visa requirements for sailboats on a monthly basis and I could never get a straight answer about their visa policies from the government agencies. Finally I decided, "I have a boat that can go anywhere I want. The Galapagos and Peru are where I really want to go, so why don't I just sail straight from Mexico to those countries?"

When I called Commander's Weather service (which is a support service that I contacted by satellite phone to get information regarding offshore weather conditions) and told them my plan, my contact person, Olivier, replied, "We don't often have boats travelling that route because of the strong Humboldt Current, so perhaps you can give us a report on the conditions! That said, there's no reason to believe that you'll have adversity, as long as you have enough fuel to fight the current." I knew that *Precious Metal* holds 500 gallons of fuel and the Humboldt Current would only take two days to cross therefore it was still a lot faster and shorter to take my chosen route over the traditional options.

Provisioning food and boat supplies for this voyage required extensive planning insofar as I was feeding three people for approximately one month and knew that the stores at the half-way point in the Galapagos were relatively basic. I began sourcing Huatulco's local butchers and food suppliers a week before our departure. One day, at a fairly primitive local butcher shop, I was explaining my situation to two delightful young Mexican men – Carlos and Juan. They keenly offered to assist me by driving me to all of the best food supply stores as well as a frozen food wholesale supplier where I purchased the bulk of my meat and fish. They also insisted that they were qualified chefs and convinced me that they could prepare the first three nights of dinners that didn't need to be frozen. This made wonderful sense to me, since I barely had time to get through my 'To Do' list prior to our departure. What was I thinking?

Several days later Carlos and Juan eagerly arrived at my boat with big smiles and a sampler of one of the dinners they intended to prepare for our first night at sea: iguana tamales – which was a chopped up iguana (complete with the eyeballs and leather skin) wrapped in palm leaves and topped with a spicy tomato sauce! I explained to them that during the first few days at sea people are prone to seasickness until they adjust to the motion of the swells. Iguana may not be the best choice for our first evening at sea. They insisted that their prized iguana dish would pass the seasickness test, although I wasn't as confident. I reluctantly agreed to try it and shared the dish at a cocktail party that evening aboard my friends' (Tom and Eliza) boat named *Alegria*. While it was a great conversation piece, only the bravest souls had a nibble. The last words that Tom said as I was parting were, "Pamela, next time we'll supply the appetizers." We all had a good laugh.

Needless to say, I contacted Carlos and Juan specifying that their iguana was very special; however, comfort food like chicken, pasta and fish are preferable for our three prepared dishes. "No problemo," they said (although I wasn't completely assured that they understood) and promised to be on the dock with our meals early morning on our specified departure date of March 15.

It's hard to imagine a more competent, accommodating and mellow person to have aboard as crew than Doug. His first question to me as we sat down to a lovely dinner in Huatulco's finest restaurants was, "Pamela, what bugs you?" I studied his question as I took a sip of my first glass of Merlot. "I mean as crew. What are the things that crew do that bother you most?"

"What an intuitive question," I replied. "Let's see: flailing sails and leaving the countertop ring handles open on the fridge."

We both smiled, toasted to our pending voyage together and continued the evening exchanging sea stories. Admittedly, Doug and I knew very little about each other prior to our voyage. He had moored his boat *Iona* at our marina in Port Hardy for short periods during the summers. He was an American living in Chile, South America, where he worked as a mechanical engineer in the mining business.

Jim, the other crew member, needed no introduction. He had helped me sail *Precious Metal* down the west coast of United States. Jim arrived on schedule bright and early the following morning, as did Carlos and Juan with our containers of meals. After storing the provisions below, there were sad farewells to my dockside friends and we cast our lines for the high seas.

We got off to a great start sailing most of the first two days and clocking an average of seven knots. A strong weather system was located to the west of us which we were trying to dodge by heading slightly eastward across the Gulf of Tehuantepec – approximately 200 miles from shore. The Gulf of Tehuantepec gave us strong offshore winds until we were approximately 200 miles due south of El Salvador. At this point we headed south and were literally able to steer by lining the mast up with the Southern Cross at night.

Carlos and Juan provided us with wonderful laughter but very little to eat on our first three evenings. While none of us was seasick, the grotesque dishes they prepared did little for our appetites. Our first mystery meal turned out to be a rabbit: heads, eyes and all, cooked amongst some nondescript vegetables that weren't suitable for human consumption. Jim's humour was at its best as he tried to pick apart the two eyeballs that were glaring up at him from his plate. After several attempts to manage a few mouthfuls we donated the meal to King Neptune and resorted to grilled cheese sandwiches which were overwhelmingly welcomed. Needless to say, we were all leery of opening meal number two the following evening. We believe it was a fish stew but we will never ever know as King Neptune devoured it as well as meal number three after taking a peek into the containers. Carlos and Juan did their best and brought us tremendous entertainment, if nothing else.

The closer we got to the Equator, the less wind we had for sailing. The band of weather stretching across the Equator is called the ITCZ (Inter-tropical Convergence Zone) and is notorious for strong squalls, torrential rains, lightning and minimal wind – also referred to as the doldrums. It's a convergence of weather systems from the northern and southern hemispheres that often collide to form a low pressure system. We experienced a number of squalls; however, they were minimal in comparison to some of horrific tales we had heard from other sailors that had endured these events. The heat became almost unbearable during the days. As part of our daily routine we stopped the boat and had a refreshing swim in order to cool off, even though the water was almost as warm as the air! One person was always on board while two would swim; naturally we tied ourselves onto *Precious Metal* with long lines.

Fishing became a preoccupation for both Jim and Doug. Each day their attempts to catch a meal created tremendous excitement. They were so successful that our standards became more demanding as each day passed. In time we began releasing most of our catches in favour of Mahi Mahi and Albacore Tuna which we decided was superior to Yellow Fin Tuna and Snapper. Consequently, our frozen meats were abandoned in lieu of the ocean's bounty of delectable fresh fish cooked in a variety of ways each evening. Several keen booby birds dove and snagged our hooks which broke our hearts. Fortunately we were able to release them unscathed and watched them fly away praying that the damage wasn't life threatening.

We all jumped to attention at the sound of the fishing line racing out of Jim or Doug's reel. They would routinely scramble to get the net and bucket and managed to bring the fish aboard, while I ran the boat and took photos of our prize. Fortunately, Doug was a master at filleting fish and within minutes of landing a catch, we were relishing the taste of fresh sashimi on the bow – complete with soy sauce and wasabi. The fish we caught ranged in size from seven to 20 pounds and every morsel was devoured with a gratifying sense of satisfaction and the comforting knowledge that we could sustain ourselves by living off the sea. My log book reads, "Jim catches the fish, Doug cleans and I cook!" I will always cherish these fond memories as one of the ultimate highs of ocean living.

Our nights also brought excitement. Phosphorescent luminescence in the tropical oceans can be mesmerizing. The high

Doug and I posing with one of our biggest catches

concentration of phosphorescent plankton in the ocean lights up whatever activity involves churning the seawater including the wake created by the boat, as well as all of the surrounding sea life. At times during the night, hundreds of porpoises would swim and jump out of the water around the boat creating a scene similar to a vibrant fireworks display. Silver silhouettes of large fish are visible swimming under and around the boat's hull. There are numerous entries in my log book referring to the spectacular nights at sea when the phosphorescence was spellbinding.

Tiny flying fish and squid are also busy at night. They can jump as high as the deck and sometimes even land inside the boat. One night Jim was sleeping soundly in the main salon bunk because his forward bunk was too hot. A flying fish came through the top hatch of the boat and landed on his pillow six inches from his head. Another six inches and it would have landed in his mouth!

Star-gazing has always been one of my favourite pastimes during night watches. On a perfect night the skies are electrified with shooting stars, brilliantly twinkling stars, meteorites, planets and a multitude of constellations that I try to identify using the numerous reference guides aboard. Entire night watches have been consumed by creating our own stories about the various constellations that have become more obscure as the voyages progressed.

A dozen booby birds decided to hitch-hike aboard *Precious Metal* during our voyage, landing one by one on the lifelines at the bow. The first few had room on the pulpit – which is a sizeable piece of stainless steel that they can wrap their claws around. The late-comers weren't as fortunate and were forced to balance on the much smaller wire lifelines that are about the size of a plug-in computer cable. As the huge sea swells rocked *Precious Metal* up and down and pitched the bow into the sea, these relentless birds tenaciously held on with their claws while being submerged with each oncoming wave. As they rose out of the water they frantically began shaking their heads just in time to be submerged again by the oncoming wave. This bird episode was truly hilarious and kept us entertained for hours and hours.

Riley's 'wake me up when we get there' character was a testimony to his wonderful nature as a boat dog. He managed another 60-hour stint of control before he finally meandered onto the bow to do his business. Once again, he received a huge round of applause and cheers as he briskly returned to the cockpit with a little skip in his gait.

Our one and only intense discussion aboard related to garbage disposal at sea. Jim, Doug and I share earnest environment philosophies and are vigilant in our lifestyles with regards to preserving our oceans and precious planet. I try to keep garbage to a minimum by throwing leftover food scraps overboard and segregating non-biodegradable items such as plastics, paper and glass. Our philosophies differed with regards to tin cans (beer and soft drinks).

Doug and I adamantly believed that tin cans decompose faster in the ocean then at a land fill or, in the case of less developed cultures, a garbage dump. Jim disagreed wholeheartedly. After further research the winner was Jim. Apparently there is not enough oxygen in the deeper depths of the ocean to decompose tin quickly. Furthermore, the cans create an unnatural habitat for the marine life that occupies the ocean floor. With thanks to Jim, I now cut the tops off my cans and use them as containers for paint and other liquids when I'm doing my maintenance. *

On the morning of Day 8, a tiny dark dot suddenly appeared on the horizon directly ahead of us. It was the first of the 19 islands and islets in the Galapagos chain. Sighting land, after eight days at sea was a rush. By 3.00pm that afternoon we were safely anchored in Isla San Christabol Harbour. The three of us were exuberant and quickly took the dinghy ashore to find our visa agent, Bolivar, so that we could clear customs and enter the country of Ecuador.

The process of checking ourselves and *Precious Metal* into the

Despite all of our efforts to separate our garbage and adhere to recycling protocol, few countries I visited during my five-year voyage are set up for proper garbage disposal. Several upscale marinas in Costa Rica practised recycling; otherwise my collection of separate garbage bags all ended up in the same bin.

Galapagos Islands took nearly a full day and $825.00 for three people. It's mandatory to use an agent and pay to obtain the various park permits. At the time of our visit, our permit allowed us to explore five specified islands, although time constraints limited us to visiting only three, including Isla San Cristobal, Isla Santa Cruz and the more remote Isla Isabela.

Doug and Jim opted to secure individual hotel rooms for the first three nights to allow us all an opportunity to spread out and for me to clean *Precious Metal*. This would be the first opportunity in eight days that we could all get a full night sleep. On our first evening, we enjoyed exploring the town of Puerto Baquerizo Moreno – which is the capital of the Galapagos province – and we treated ourselves to a terrific meal ashore. I couldn't take Riley into town because an abundance of sea lions had taken over the dinghy dock and also inhabited the main road along the ocean.

During our first night alone aboard *Precious Metal* in the Galapagos, Riley and I were sleeping soundly when I was suddenly awakened at around 3.00am. We became aware of heavy breathing and a horrible smell. My arm automatically reached for the light and to my horror I witnessed a giant sea lion entering the hatch beside my bed at a very fast pace! I screamed and whacked his nose with my book which was the only thing within a quick reach. He backed away slightly and I managed to close and lock the hatch. My heart was racing. What would I have done if he had managed to slither into my bed?

The sea lion intruder remained steadfast on my swim deck staring into the hatch window. Riley, who is known to growl twice a year (usually at his shadow), awakened during the commotion and began growling furiously at the sea lion, placing his nose against the hatch window. The sea lion began to bark back with his nose also against the outside window. This constant barking continued unabated for three hours until sunrise. The two animals were making the most grotesque noises with their noses a window pane apart. I finally calmed myself when I realized we were safe inside the boat. It was one of those ridiculous scenes when all I could do was laugh hysterically at this one of a kind bizarre incident.

During the following eight days we explored most of the three islands and managed two extensive inland hikes. Each of the islands is remarkably different in terms of scenery and local natural inhabitants. Lush beaches of powdery white sand and majestic palm trees line most of the shorelines, while a more desert-like vegetation and rocky terrain exist further inland and into the mountainous hillsides. Jim signed up for a snorkelling trip which he thoroughly enjoyed, swimming with the multitude of unique tropical fish of the region. The Charles Darwin Research Centre on Isla Santa Cruz was extremely interesting and informative and allowed us an opportunity to walk within a few feet of giant 125-year-old tortoises. Our beach walks gave us ample opportunity to see marine iguanas which are the only lizard species that are adapted for swimming. Our anchorage in Isla Isabela provided amazing photo opportunities with penguins swimming around the boat and blue-footed boobies perched regally on the shore beside us.

In hindsight, my Galapagos experience was well worth the time, money and effort. That said, it wasn't what I expected. My impressions of the Galapagos were two-fold. On the one hand, the local people are wonderfully engaging, friendly and easy-going; however, I should have been there 30 years ago. What was I thinking? Naively, after reading Charles Darwin's book and other literature, my image of the Galapagos was of an undeveloped group of islands with giant tortoises meandering along the dirt roads and a few innocuous tourist hotels nestled in the background. Instead, tourism is alive and well in these islands. Surprisingly, there are a multitude of designer stores, cruise ships, fine dining restaurants and tourist services throughout the two main islands of San Cristobal and Santa Cruz.

The Galapagos Islands face major problems with regard to their development and authorities are caught in a Catch-22 dilemma. Tourism is needed to support their extensive ecological conservation programs, yet the tourism industry itself puts

There's someone for everyone: two sexy giant iguanas frolicking on the beach

incredible stress on the delicate ecology and negates a lot of the well-meaning efforts. Since tourism first began to develop in the early 1970s a huge influx of mainland Ecuadorians have relocated to the Galapagos to help develop and support the tourism infrastructure. Our tour guide at the Charles Darwin Research Centre told us that this influx of people has increased the population at a rate of 12 percent per year. The Charles Darwin Research Centre, Darwin Scientific Foundation and Galapagos National Park Service have been instrumental in instituting strict conservation guidelines for residents and visitors over the years, yet despite their efforts, they are fighting a huge battle to preserve and maintain these Enchanted Islands.*

Our final day at Isla Isabela was spent trying to locate our agent José in order to check out of the country and obtain our Zarpe for Peru (boats are required to obtain an international Zarpe document when departing every country as this paperwork is part of clearing out procedures). Bolivar, our agent on San Cristobal had instructed us where to find José; although he

Prior to being named the Galapagos Islands, the early Spanish explorers named the archipelago Las Islas Encantadas: *The Enchanted Islands.*

A regal blue-footed booby nearby Precious Metal *at anchor off Isla Isabela*

neglected to tell us that José was away on a two-week vacation.

We walked for hours on end in circles, being directed to every José who lived on the island – all to no avail. Finally, late in the day, we met a charming man named Miguel who insisted that he could help. Together with the port captain, they both assured us that our documents were complete and issued our new Zarpe. Little did I know at the time that our trust in Miguel's knowledge would come back to haunt us when I attempted to enter mainland Ecuador seven months later.*

Over the course of our time in the Galapagos we managed to provision, re-fuel and prepare *Precious Metal* for her next voyage to Lima, Peru. A seven-day window of decent weather opened and allowed us to depart bright and early the morning of April 2. We were bound for Lima, which was to become my home for the next seven months.

* *This story to be continued in Chapter 12*

"Yahoo! We're Heading to Peru"

We cheered as we hoisted the anchor and left Isla Isabela in the distance. The beauty of sailing this next 1,100-nautical-mile leg was that everyone had become intimately familiar with the boat and knew their respective responsibilities and routines at sea. Within minutes of crossing the Galapagos' 'no fishing' boundary, both Jim and Doug quickly rigged their fishing rods. The winds were still too light for sailing which forced us to continue by motor.

By this time, I too joined in the fishing frenzy. Jim's line was off the port aft quarter, Doug's was from the starboard and my line was straight out the back of the boat. Late afternoon on our second day at sea, our biggest fish to date landed on Doug's line. After an exhilarating struggle, we hauled in a monstrous 35-pound Sierra.

Not only were Jim and Doug becoming quite adept at hoisting fish onto the boat, but they also perfected a technique that greatly reduced the amount of blood coming aboard. By placing a line around the tail and dragging the fish through the water upside-down until it was clearly dead, made it much easier to lift and clean the fish for filleting. In an attempt to be more humane we also tried pouring vodka and tequila into their gills which apparently kills the fish instantly (and presumably happily), but ultimately decided it was a waste of good booze! What were we thinking?

A new twist to this particular voyage was that the Peruvian government had very strict protocol with regards to boats entering their country. Because so few cruising boats visit Peru, they haven't established a department that handles nautical tourism and therefore every boat is treated like a commercial vessel. I was given strict instructions in advance of our voyage that as soon as I crossed into Peruvian waters I had to phone in and report to the Peruvian ship transportation department (called TRAMAR) every day at 8.00am and 8.00pm. I reluctantly agreed to execute their instructions, although at the time it seemed like a futile waste of time and expensive satellite phone minutes.

Among the many sailing organizations that I belong to, the Seven Seas Sailing Association has been the most instrumental in assisting me during this voyage as well as the two and a half years I spent cruising in the South Pacific during the late 1980s. The organization is world-wide and essentially supports cruising boats around the globe by recruiting knowledgeable representatives in most countries to use as local resources and hosts. In advance of my Peruvian voyage I contacted their Lima representative, Gonzalo Ravago, to advise him of my pending arrival. Gonzalo was incredibly helpful and emailed me a welcome package with extensive information about Peru as well as the phone number for TRAMAR.

Fortunately, I owned a satellite phone to make these calls. It's very important to record the details of these calls because they require a copy of the telephone records as part of the necessary documentations in obtaining a Peruvian entry permit. In fact, several weeks after my arrival in Peru, I met one cruising couple that had sailed all the way to Lima only to be refused entry because they neglected to provide the requisite telephone records upon arrival. Incredibly, they were instructed to sail 200 miles offshore and return again with their daily calls! I never saw them again and believe they simply bypassed Peru.

We crossed into Peruvian waters early morning on April 7 under cloudy skies and markedly cooler temperatures. The effects of the adverse Humboldt Current were beginning to slow us down so we altered course towards mainland Ecuador in order to take advantage of the prevailing southerly winds. Given that commercial vessels travel between 12 and 20 knots and take a direct route from point to point, they call TRAMAR only a couple of times before arriving in Lima. Unfortunately, the same couldn't be said for *Precious Metal* since our speed was reduced to four knots and we were taking an indirect circular route to Lima. Accordingly, our phone calls to TRAMAR became an entertaining part of our daily routine over the course of the next four days.

At this point, my knowledge of Spanish was just enough to get me into trouble. During my two years in Mexico I made a noble attempt to practice, yet many Mexicans speak English and are also trying to learn the language so I wasn't able to completely immerse myself in Spanish. Having been raised in Montreal, Quebec, I had a reasonable command of French which was helpful in understanding Spanish, although it also complicated matters because as I often got the two languages mixed up. It was clear to me on my first phone call to TRAMAR that none of the officials spoke a word of English. Furthermore, the clarity on a satellite phone from the middle of the ocean was often distorted.

Because of this language barrier, it took Marco and me over 30 minutes on my first call to establish the name of my boat, my name, a few details about the boat and crew, our speed, destination and location. Then, as the days passed our conversations became more friendly and informal. As soon as I mentioned my name, either Marco or Havier's response would be: "Okay, Okay." And they would proceed to open my file. The first questions in broken English were "How are you?" "How is your boat?" "Are you happy on your boat?" Soon, they had perfected every question in English and I tried to perfect every answer in Spanish. I truly believe that they sincerely cared about this female captain crossing their waters.

Over the course of our 11-day sail to Peru, each day at sea rolled into the next with continued camaraderie, serious cribbage games, reading, fishing, phone calls to TRAMAR, delicious fish feasts and deep discussion surrounding Jim's literary philosophies. Every time anyone attempted to do a task or chore, it was prefaced with the phrase: "Okay, Okay!"– followed by some genuine laughter. At times during our eighth and ninth day when the intensity of the Humboldt Current was the greatest, our speed was reduced to three knots and we feared that Jim would miss his flight home on April 12. Suddenly on our 10th day *Precious Metal* regained her speed as we raced towards Lima at seven knots. Having more than doubled our speed overnight, we felt like we were driving in a race car!

With 20 miles remaining to Lima Harbour, my final call into TRAMAR at 8.00am on April 11 was classic. I believe it was Marco who answered my call and in addition to his usual questions, he provided me with navigational directions into the harbour. Finally, when I thanked him and mentioned it was my last call he replied, "Welcome to my World" in perfect English. Marcos and Havier as well as the other officials at TRAMAR were incredibly endearing and provided a wonderful introduction to Peru.

A huge, black cloud descended on us shortly after my final TRAMAR call obliterating all visibility of land ahead. It seemed a shame that we finally had land in sight and then had to navigate strictly by radar for most of the 20 miles into Lima. Our instructions were to proceed to a marker at Mile 14 and then radio the port authorities for further instructions. Numerous freighters and large commercial vessels passed us in each direction making navigation by radar incredibly difficult and intense. At Mile 14 we were told to proceed to a marker at Mile 9. We ventured slowly with someone on the deck at all times and sounding our horn every two minutes. At Mile 9 we were given clearance to enter into the harbour and were essentially on our own to navigate between the ships at anchor and those under way.

Suddenly, as we rounded the corner into the harbour, a sailboat under full sail was approaching us on a collision course. Every time I altered course to let it pass, it would also alter course and head directly towards us. I admit to becoming increasingly frustrated.

Finally, when the sailboat was so close that I had nowhere to turn I pulled back on the throttle to stop the boat. The sailboat jibbed completely around followed by a huge commotion of waving and cheering in our direction. It was Gonzalo Ravago and his family coming out to greet us and usher us into the Peruano Yacht Club. We couldn't have had a warmer welcome. This was just the beginning of the incredible hospitality that Gonzalo, his lovely wife Magdella, two wonderful children (Gonzalo and Magdella Jr) and his entire extended family provided during my seven unbelievable months in their country.

We were also greeted by Jaime, the Peruano Yacht Club manager and safely secured *Precious Metal* onto a mooring buoy.

After some short introductions, a water taxi arrived and shuttled us into the prestigious yacht club that overlooks the harbour. Seconds later, we were served highly potent pisco sours which are Peruvian traditional drinks. Knowing the potency, Doug and I only drank one glass. Jim, on the other hand had three! I believe that the rest of the evening was history for Jim, although he was highly entertaining and jokingly threatened to dive off of the restaurant balcony truly believing that he could swim back to Canada!

We celebrated the balance of the evening in style, tasting an endless stream of amazing and delicious Peruvian specialities emerging from Chef Frano's kitchen. It was a bitter-sweet ending for me because my crew was departing the following day and I was dreading having to say good-bye. That said, I was also becoming tougher knowing that when one door closes, another one opens. I was confident that the upcoming chapter in my life would be one of a lifetime. Peru lived up to all of my expectations and more. In fact, it leapfrogged over Italy and Bhutan to become my favourite country to visit in the world!

CHAPTER 10

Peru: Another Dream Come True

April 11, 2010

D ESPITE THE ENORMOUS fanfare surrounding our arrival into Peru, my first few days after Jim and Doug's departure were incredibly depressing and lonely. Suddenly, my friends were gone and the highs from our ocean passage were over. I was in a strange country and didn't speak the language. I was moored in the tiny town of La Punta which was a 30-minute drive into Lima and there were no fellow cruising boats in the anchorage. The surrounding skies were completely grey and overcast. The reality of knowing that I was in Peru with my boat for at least seven months before the next window of good weather would open hit me hard. What was I thinking? Should I have stayed in Mexico?

I dedicated my first day in Lima to cleaning *Precious Metal* and awoke the second day with slightly more vigour. I knew that I needed to change my attitude and make a plan to enjoy Peru – a country that I worked so hard to get to, not to mention the fact that it was my lifelong dream. Also, I needed to go ashore and get food and supplies. By late afternoon on my second day of pouting, I committed to a new plan that would allow me to get immersed into the country.

My plan was to dedicate two hours each day towards learning Spanish by simply walking Riley through the streets and shops and trying to engage in conversation. In addition, I would use this time on my own to begin writing my second book which was long overdue. But first, I needed to do what every woman is entitled to after a month-long ocean passage: get my nails and hair done!

I awoke to a huge ray of sunshine illuminating my cabin. This was the first sign of the sun since arriving in Peru so I leaped out of bed to take advantage of the warm and brilliant light. I made myself a cup of coffee and relaxed in the cockpit, taking stock of my surroundings and what would be my new home for the next seven months. My first observation was the incredible number of beautiful boats moored on buoys throughout the yacht club boundary. Interestingly, some of the mooring buoys had electrical outlets for power to their respective boats which was something I had never seen before.

As I peered through my binoculars taking in 360 degrees of my surroundings it almost felt like home in as much as all of the Peruvian flags on the adjacent vessels were almost identical to Canada's flag except the Canadian flag has a maple leaf in the centre. "I guess no one is going to know we're visitors," I said to Riley. "Our flag looks almost the same as Peru's and doesn't stand out at all in the midst of these Peruvian flags."

As I looked towards the shoreline, the charming little town of La Punta was to my right and appeared to be reasonably upscale. To my left was the industrial port of Callao which Jaime and Gonzalo warned me was very unsafe. "There is tremendous crime, often drug related and few police in Callao. Never walk there alone and take a taxi when you need to go in that direction," advised Jaime.

I drank my second cup of coffee while searching through my Spanish–English dictionary for the words to say, "Where can I find a place to get my nails done?" "*Donde es un tienda para dedo?*" The dictionary didn't include fingernail so I settled for *dedo* which means finger and I planned to point to my nails. It seemed pretty straight forward to me. What was I thinking?

The yacht club seemed to anticipate my call when I radioed

for the water taxi service, because within minutes Agusto was alongside my boat ready to pick up Riley and me. Agusto was incredibly respectful and took my hand to assist me into his boat as well as help in collecting a few bags of garbage.

Octavio, the restaurant manager was waiting for me as I climbed the ramp onto the main dock and greeted me in a professional and courteous manner. After our initial pleasantries, I pointed to my fingernails and politely asked him, "*Donde es un teinda para dedo?*" Octavio's face went into shock! He was frantic and began yelling at me in Spanish before disappearing into the restaurant's back door to the kitchen. I was totally perplexed since I had no idea what I did or said that could be so incredibly offensive and cause such a reaction.

I could hear Octavio and Chef Frano (who is bilingual) sharing harsh words in the kitchen and I patiently waited outside wondering what it was that I said. Finally the two men emerged from the kitchen and approached me. Frano stood at attention with his hands behind his back and said in a very frank voice, "Pamela, you just asked the restaurant manager where to find a store that sells dildos and if you ask this on the street you will find yourself in a very bad part of town in a sex store!" I was aghast.

Never, ever in my life have I been so embarrassed. I thought I was going to die. I explained to Frano that I practised my sentence early this morning and wanted to get my nails done. "I understand this Pamela, but apparently you pronounced the vowel 'e' incorrectly. We suggest that from now on you practice your questions with us before leaving the Yacht Club!"

Frano politely directed me to a beauty salon in town and I slinked away virtually in tears. "How do they like me so far?" I said to myself shaking my head. What were they thinking? There I was, this blonde Canadian woman, arriving from nearly a month at sea and after two days of isolation aboard her boat the first question she asks is, "Where can I find a dildo?" It took tremendous courage to walk back through the yacht club after my nails were done but I had no choice – I had to confront the situation. I even considered swimming back to my boat directly from shore to avoid the Yacht Club. By the time I returned, Frano was making a joke of the incident and we both had a good laugh. We agreed that this was the ultimate ice-breaker and still laugh about it today. As for Octavio, I don't believe that he found the incident as humorous.

Before long, Riley and I settled into a wonderful new lifestyle and daily routine in our safe little town of La Punta. Each morning we would take a long walk around the perimeter of the town and soon most of the local merchants and residents were participating in my quest to learn Spanish. Riley received enormous attention as he paraded down the street. The security guards that patrolled the streets of La Punta loved Riley and after asking Riley's age on numerous occasions I made them aware of Riley's birthday. To my surprise Riley was not only greeted with a fanfare of birthday greetings from the guards on his birthday, but Frano cooked him a wonderful steak dinner in the restaurant as well!

My afternoons were devoted towards writing this book, which has had many lives since then, but it all began in Peru. In the late afternoon, Riley and I would take a short walk and then I would indulge in some of Frano's wonderful feasts for dinner. Peruvian food has so many unique, wonderful tastes that aren't found anywhere else in the world. Gonzalos and his delightful wife Magdella often invited me to their Sunday family meals or out to dinner in the city. Their two children were equally engaging and friendly as well as their entire extended family. The hospitality was wonderfully heart-warming. It was as if no one could do enough for us.

My only criticism of Lima and the surrounding area was that the water was particularly dirty and the skies were generally grey from clouds and smog. The combination of the Humboldt Current, effecting cloud formations and the fact that Callao is a large busy port with constant freighter traffic arriving and departing helps to explain why these conditions exist. One only needs to venture a few miles inland from the city to find beautiful sunshine and stunning countryside. What concerned me was that Lima wasn't the only location where water and air pollution seemed irreparable. The water in most of the major coastal towns in Mexico was unfit for swimming and vast expanses of garbage were lining the shores as well as floating in the sea. The label on the water-maker filters says to change them every six months, yet mine were filthy after just a few uses. "What's really going on?" I wondered.

My writing in Peru began by researching and contacting the various oceanographic agencies throughout the world in an effort to understand whether there is, in fact, a crisis. While the majority of these agencies were overwhelmingly responsive to my questions and concerns, the gist of their replies remained the same, "It's a lot worse than you think." I thoroughly researched the subject of sea and air pollution, reading and trying to absorb everything I could find on the topic in an effort to ensure that my facts were accurate.

Surprisingly, many of these agencies focus on one particular aspect of the oceans (fishing, coral reefs, climate change, pollution, etc) and there was very little available that consolidated the entire picture relating to all of the issues affecting every ocean. Furthermore, I discovered that most of these organizations are either volunteer, or get by on minimal budgets and are consequently limited in the scope of their research due to lack of funding. It's not surprising that little is truly known about the seriousness of our ocean crisis.*

Despite my enthusiasm for Peru, Ilver was unable to leave his development business to join me so I decided to return to Canada for June, July and August to be with him in Port Hardy as well as visit my friends in Canada. I had one objective before

---

This book is meant to be an entertaining sailing story and not an in-depth scientific journal. While my concerns for the oceans are real, my intentions are to heighten awareness while leaving the facts to scientific and marine specialists. My readings and research that derived to the above conclusions were extensive. Most notably, the book entitled, Seasick: The Global Ocean in Crisis by Alanna Mitchell (McClelland & Stewart Ltd, 2009) was the most informed, powerful and passionate account of the accelerating crisis in our oceans. I attribute many of my conclusions to this important, educational and riveting 'must read' book.

departing Peru, which was to see Macchu Pichu and do a trek in the Andes Mountains. Gonzalo introduced me to his reputable travel adviser named Pepe who was able to instantly put together a 10-day expedition that included both destinations.

I frantically canvassed everyone I knew at the yacht club to find a home for Riley during those 10 days. The only keen responder was Agusto, the water-taxi driver. Knowing that Agusto lived in a tiny village in the distant hills behind Lima, I knew that Riley wouldn't be spoiled in the same fashion as he was with me. Nonetheless, I was confident that he would be loved by all of the villagers and be the centre of attention for the children. I conjured visions of my spoiled Riley sleeping in a tiny hut laden with goats, chickens, scrawny wild dogs and waking up each morning to the resident rooster calls. "Riley, this won't be Kansas," I said during our parting cuddle. "We're both going on a new Peruvian adventure and I think that yours will be even greater than mine!"

Both Macchu Pichu and the Andes Mountains far exceeded my expectations. The ancient Inca civilization of Macchu Pichu is simply breath-taking. In contrast to my three prior Himalaya treks in Nepal and Bhutan, which I thoroughly enjoyed, the Salkantay Trail, which runs parallel to the Inca Trail, was far less developed and showed few signs of tourism. I joined a fantastic group of seven people from many corners of the globe. The weather was superb, the scenery was stunning and each night our pristine lodges nestled into the mountains were absolutely first class.

As we meandered through the indigenous mountain villages full of genuinely proud and curious inhabitants, I half expected to find Riley lying on a dirt path devouring a guinea pig carcass or basking in the mud beside a hog. What was I thinking? Despite my utmost respect and confidence in Agusto, how could I have left my precious little baby for 10 whole days in such extreme conditions compared to his life of virtual royalty aboard *Precious Metal*?

I returned to *Precious Metal* on schedule after my expedition

My single-handed hand-stand as a single-handed sailor with the breath-taking ancient city of Macchu Pichu in the background

and found Agusto giving Riley a bath in the cockpit. This led me to believe that it was Riley's first bath in 10 days and wondered what he looked like before I arrived. I regretted not leaving a camera with Agusto to give me some idea of Riley's lifestyle during my absence. Except for a few ticks which were easily removed, Riley was healthy and happy to see me. "If only you could talk to me just this once, to tell me about your experience," I said to him. Riley's 10 days of existence in a remote Peruvian village will always remain a mystery although I would give anything to know what he was thinking living in such a foreign environment.

The Peruano Yacht Club offered a completely different

scenario when I returned to Lima early the following September. Nine cruising boats were moored around me, all destined for Chile and rounding Cape Horn. Gonzalo's family, Chef Frano and my fellow cruisers continuously hosted fun cocktail hours, breakfast, brunches and evenings out in the big city of Lima. I felt completely at ease with my location and by then had acquired a reasonable command of the Spanish language.

Upon reflection, the types of cruisers heading to Chile are unique to sailors that frequent more convenient regions such as Mexico and North America. I found these sailors to be hardier, with both partners completely committed to cruising. There was little doubt that many of my new-found friends were not second-guessing their quest of rounding Cape Horn; rather, they were keen to be put to the test.

Late in September I organized a 'ladies' luncheon' at one of the posh restaurants in downtown Lima so that we could all enjoy some girl-time. While my intentions were innocent, this lunch became a major turning point in my life. Our group of nine courageous and interesting women sat down in random places around the table and began sipping pisco sours – which were so tasty that we enjoyed a second round. I was sitting beside a woman named Edi who I barely knew before that day although she seemed very friendly. We began discussing how we had arrived at this point in our lives on our sailboats in Peru. Edi was in her early 60s and had met her husband Mike only a few years earlier. Several years ago she had answered an advertisement that Mike had posted soliciting crew and the rest was history. It was love at first sight.

My story was much more complicated. Edi learned that I was torn between my love for this cruising environment that was my lifetime dream, versus the life I had created with my partner Ilver in the tiny remote community of Port Hardy. While I had tremendous love and respect for Ilver, his wonderful family and everything he represented, our passions were so opposed. I had discovered during my recent three months in Port Hardy that I had little in common with most of the local residents and

Ilver had little in common with my sailing community. What was I thinking? How could a woman who had visited over 100 countries in the world and intended to continue exploring the planet by boat relate with people who so dearly loved their tiny enclave of Port Hardy? Conversely, how could Ilver and his friends relate to me? No one was to blame; we were simply on different paths in life.

The best illustration of our disparity in values was at lunch with a group of women during my first visit back to Port Hardy (after nine months of cruising). An hour into the conversation, one woman addressed me asking, "Pamela, have you been away?" "Yes," I replied. "I sailed my boat from Mexico to Peru." I sensed that she wasn't able to comprehend the magnitude of my statement or the voyage when she replied, "Oh and where did you leave your car?"

Edi was completely understanding and articulated her philosophy in life. "Pamela, you and I and the women at this lunch have always lived outside of the box. We don't conform to the norms of our society. Sure, every once in a while we jump back inside the box and do everything in our power to conform because we dream of being normal. We find a partner, settle into a nice home and try to build our futures in our community, but eventually we become impatient and begin wanting to escape the box. Eventually the box begins to suffocate us, because the people around us don't relate and vice versa."

A huge lump developed in my stomach as I digested Edi's out-of-the-box theory. Knowing that her philosophies of life resonated with me and recognizing that she was right in her thinking meant that I had a tough choice to make. "Out of the box people need to become partners with other people from the outside," she exclaimed. The remainder of my luncheon was overshadowed with the sad reality that my life as I knew it with Ilver and Port Hardy was about to change. And it did.*

Sadly, nine months following my separation from Ilver he suffered a tragic accident which has rendered him a paraplegic. My thoughts and prayers will always be with him.

As I sailed further away from Canada, major holidays often raised a sense of homesickness and reminded me of how far away I was from my homeland. Canadian Thanksgiving was no exception. I awoke on our Thanksgiving morning feeling a strong sense of nostalgia as friends and families shared their intentions of their pending turkey dinners on the Internet. That morning I asked Chef Frano whether he had turkey on the menu for that evening and he replied, "No, but we'll find you some. Meet me here at 6.00pm and we'll go into the city to celebrate!" Joe, a captain on another boat in the bay also agreed to join us. What was I thinking? Apparently turkey is not a Peruvian favourite.

That night we drove and drove around the city in search of some turkey and struck out completely. By 8.00pm we had canvassed every restaurant that Frano and Joe knew existed and every owner shook their head with regret. Finally, Frano drove to his family home where his traditional Peruvian family was gathered in the living room including his parents, grandparents, uncles, aunts, nieces and nephews all engaged in animated conversation. The room went silent when Frano entered and explained the problem. Immediately after explaining our predicament, every adult in the room brought out their cell phones and began dialling familiar restaurants. I was awe-struck witnessing at least five adults relentlessly phoning around the city in rapid Spanish in their noble quest to find my turkey.

Finally, one man cheered! Success! After some discussion, he advised the restaurant that we would be arriving in 15 minutes and to hold the turkey for us. There was huge fanfare as we bid our farewell and rushed out of the door. When we arrived at the restaurant, we were greeted as though we were royalty. Waiters appeared from every corner of the room to shake our hands and usher us to our table. After scoping out the room, it was evident that the restaurant was more like a corner diner with plastic tables, chairs and utensils, yet the proprietor's genuine hospitality and effort to please us made up for the lack of ambiance.

This establishment didn't serve wine so Frano suggested that they run to the local grocery store for some *vino*. They returned with a half bottle of a no-name white. Within minutes of our arrival they proudly proceeded to serve my turkey dinner which consisted of a Caesar salad in a plastic bowl with sandwich strips of processed turkey! I had to smile. While it could never compare to a traditional Thanksgiving feast, the warmth and wonderful intentions of so many people contributed to a truly memorable occasion and a Thanksgiving that I will never forget.

My visit to the dentist to have my teeth cleaned was equally unforgettable. The attractive young dentist that I was referred to appeared appropriately professional. He spoke very little English, but, then again, no one really chats in a dentist chair. Before he proceeded to clean my teeth he pointed to the screen above my head and asked if I wanted to watch a movie. What a wonderful way to endure a dental appointment I thought and nodded in agreement. During the film's introduction, it appeared that the young dentist had even gone out of his way to provide an English speaking film. What he probably didn't realize was that this film was a semi-porn soap opera! Dental appointments don't get any better than this one – looking directly into the eyes of a gorgeous young Peruvian male while watching a quasi-porn movie! Believe me, I didn't feel any pain.

In October of that season, I was part of an incredible inland excursion down the Amazon River and exploration of the Amazon Rainforest. This grand finale with six other meaningful friends from Canada and the United States epitomized the very best in Peruvian scenery, hospitality and culture. I was so fortunate to enjoy the very finest of Peru and cherish so many terrific memories.

All good things must come to an end, but saying good-bye to Peru seemed to cut deeper into my heart. My friend Barry (from the sailing vessel *Eagle*) agreed to join me in Lima and assist in bringing *Precious Metal* to Central America. After endless hours of preparations and good-byes, we were ready to set sail on November 15. Gonzalo was as hospitable as ever on my day of departure. In addition to a grand farewell party for all the departing boats, a huge package of wonderful gifts was awaiting me at the yacht club on my final day in Peru. It was with tremendous sadness that I choked back my tears and bid farewell to my new Peruvian friends whom I will always remember for their incredible hospitality, warmth and generosity.

Ocean Crisis

During this voyage, the shocking deterioration of our oceans made a tremendous impact on me. Simply stated, our oceans are a mess and the marine life as well as our entire planet are facing serious consequences if we don't immediately address and deal with this crisis.*

I believe that it takes living on the ocean for prolonged periods of time to appreciate fully the magnitude of the problem. After all, why would people on land seriously concern themselves with our oceans when there are so many land-based distractions? Furthermore, the perception that our oceans are so vast and seemingly plentiful lends itself to the belief that Mother Nature will overcome any and all catastrophes. The oceans are the lungs and sustenance of our planet. Oceans can live very happily without humans, but humans can't live without oceans.

Simply stated, all life on our planet depends on our oceans. Our oceans provide us with over 50 percent of the oxygen we breathe – more than our tropical rainforests. Due to the ocean's depth, marine life represents 99 percent of life on our planet whereas human life on land represents one percent. Humans, (theoretically the most intelligent species) occupy a tiny one percent of land – yet our behaviour could be contributing to the fatality of our entire planet.

Being the eternal optimist, I admit that the bigger picture didn't faze me for quite a while during this voyage. Yet, like a sore that never heals, I became concerned. I've become increasingly aware that our harbours and nearby waters and rivers are filthy; it's tougher to catch fish; the fish seem so much smaller; the coral

---

*Appendix II, If Fish Could Talk, *is an article I wrote based on a presentation I give to groups around the world.*

reefs seem harder to find and most have little life; and garbage is everywhere – lining every pristine beach, floating on the ocean and lying the ocean floor everywhere I swim and snorkel. My water-maker filters should last six months. Now I have to change them every two to three weeks because of thick, black gooey crud being filtered out of the water. There are red tides, brown tides and an abundance of jelly fish floating everywhere (jelly fish are considered the cockroaches of the ocean).

My concern for our oceans went to greater depth and became somewhat of an obsession this year. Is what I'm witnessing indicative of a serious ocean crisis? Due to my lifelong love for the ocean, I immersed myself in every piece of research available. I'm not a marine biologist, nor a scientist, but one doesn't need to be a specialist in this field to know that something's amiss.

The first realization from my research was that while we have a number of highly reputable researchers (oceanographers, marine biologists, meteorologists and the like) studying the oceans; on a relative scale they're only scratching the surface and they admit to many unanswered questions. The marine systems are so massive, complex and interconnected that it takes a monumental amount of qualified resources to comprehend the entire scenario. Furthermore, everything they're studying and the problems we are facing with regard to the deterioration of our oceans is unprecedented – these circumstances have never existed since man inhabited the planet roughly 200,000 years ago. Yet given the scope of the problem, what is more distressing is the fact that this ocean crisis began relatively recently.

Societies spend enormous amounts of funding on research of human illnesses and yet the lungs and sustenance of our planet are in jeopardy and need to become a priority. Based on my research our major concerns include:

1. Concentrated carbon emissions from our atmosphere are changing the acidity balance of the sea water which affects many species of marine life including plankton (which

produce our oxygen) and coral reefs.

2. Global warming is altering the water levels, temperatures and weather systems, causing major redistribution of marine life and preventing photosynthesis of our coral reefs.
3. Pollution and garbage from humans tamper with the chemical balances of the sea water and are causing catastrophic ramifications for marine life.
4. Over-fishing is seriously depleting the fish stock and other species that depend on fish for survival – including humans, birds and animals.
5. Sloppy tourism practices in pristine tropical regions are devastating our coral reefs which host over 25% of our sea life.
6. Low oxygen 'dead zones' from land usage (and other unknown reasons) are being discovered in many prominent ocean regions including the Gulf of Mexico and Humboldt Current (406 have been identified to date).

Each of these crises is extremely serious individually. Added together they place enormous stress on all living species. While our oceans are incredibly versatile and resilient, their capacity to withstand further devastation is still a major concern.

Garbage is the single-most horrifying issue for me as a cruiser and it's something that we can all rectify with education and by taking responsibility for our planet. While recycling has become a way of life for most westernized countries, it is merely a band-aid. Why are plastics and Styrofoam containers even permitted to be manufactured? Our governments need to take strict action on the types of packaging that suppliers and manufacturers use and produce. Virtually everything we buy in the stores is packaged in wasteful containers that are simply discarded as soon as we open the product.

Globalization has made huge in-roads into many facets of our societies and yet there has been little done globally to rectify the inequality between environmental behaviours of developing and developed countries around the world. When

119

I've visited developed countries, I'm appalled at the waste due to consumption and industry. Conversely, the developing countries I've visited display minimal consumption relative to the First World; however, they are too poorly educated and equipped to address environmental issues. If governments of westernized countries truly want a cleaner global environment they need to reach out to assist the impoverished countries. We all share the same air and oceans.

Our environmental issues will never be solved without a meaningful, effective global strategy.

CHAPTER 11

Ecuador: The Good, the Bad and the Ugly

November 2010

THE SADNESS OF casting off my mooring lines from the Peruano Yacht Club was enormously painful and quite a tearjerker. The reality of knowing that this seven-month experience was, in all likelihood, a once-in-a-lifetime event and that I would probably never see these wonderful people again tormented me for the better part of my first day at sea. One of the greatest challenges of cruising life has been bidding farewell to so many wonderful people who have provided unforgettable experiences and warm relationships. I've always hated saying good-bye.

With my long-time friend Barry aboard as crew, we set sail northbound from Lima towards Ecuador and the ultimate goal of reaching Panama in a month's time. Knowing that several cruising friends were hosting a traditional (US) Thanksgiving party during the third week of November in Puerto Amasted (700 miles to the north), our plan was to stop for a week or two in mainland Ecuador before setting sail another 500 miles to Panama.

My melancholy state did not last long. On our first day at sea Barry decided to turn on the stereo. I immediately noticed that my voltage meter was not charging at the normal level, despite the fact that we were running the engine, and the stereo was rapidly consuming our amperage hours. My 200 amp alternator (which charges the batteries) had been repaired in Lima earlier in the week by a reliable mechanic so this new ominous electrical problem was a mystery. What was I thinking? When the alternator was re-installed (and presumably repaired) I was plugged into electrical power and never thought to test the new repairs. I simply relied on the skills and knowledge of the local mechanic who assured me it was working well.

We immediately reduced the amount of power being consumed and tried to figure out why the battery was not charging. After many fruitless hours exhausting all possible remedies to fix the problem – including contacting mechanically savvy friends on the satellite phone – it was determined that the regulator in my main alternator was faulty. Apparently the mechanic installed a faulty regulator instead of repairing it. Furthermore, because of the absence of Honda dealers in Lima, I could not service my back-up portable Honda generator and therefore we had no ability to charge the batteries. The solar panels generally supply enough power to maintain the refrigerator and lights, but as luck would have it we had no sun.

We were instantly in a crisis mode and had to assess our dire situation. Returning to Lima was not a preferred option for several reasons: I had already checked out of Peru and the procedures for re-entering the country were onerous and costly (a new 'agriculture charge' had recently been enforced raising the total re-entry amount to over $800.00.); the mooring facilities at the Peruano Yacht Club didn't have a dock to re-charge batteries which would be needed while I waited for the repair; we had already sailed over 150 miles and psychologically wanted to continue making progress. Our closest port with the facilities to obtain power was in Salinas, Ecuador, the southernmost corner of the country – another 450 nautical miles north.

Regrettably, this new situation forced me to essentially shut down all of the systems that required power. I estimated that using a bare bones amount of power for the navigation lights and refrigerator, our consumption would be approximately 50 amperage hours a day, which was just enough to get us to Salinas. I could turn off the refrigerator as a last resort if my calculations were incorrect. Accordingly, for the following five days we managed to survive at sea without the use of any pumps, lights or amenities that require power. We were forced to refrain from running the water, playing music and most electronic navigation was shut off. Needless to say, it was an exceedingly long and stressful five days.

Manual steering is a sailor's nightmare and is particularly challenging at night along the north Peruvian and southern Ecuadorian coastline. Regardless of our distance offshore, the fishermen who operated off the coast at night created major hazardous conditions and cause for concern for sailors. In fact, I eventually decided not to use my sails at night because the fishermen made it impossible to stay on a proper course.

Typically, just before dusk the fishermen would head out to sea in their primitive open-air outboard motor boats and stake their fishing territory for the night. They used long lines to mark their territory, identified by rudimentary plastic floating containers (milk jugs, Coke bottles) or household objects. It was imperative that we stay clear of these fishing lines or they would get caught in the propeller or wrapped around the keel. Furthermore, these fishermen often slept in their boats with their only source of light being a flashlight. State-of-the-art radar systems would be able to identify these boats; however, mine could not identify such minute detail.

The chaos and stress would begin every night just after sunset. *Precious Metal* would casually be motoring along when suddenly a light would begin to flash at us and a panicked Peruvian fisherman would start screaming in his native language. I sensed that we likely awoke and startled them because our navigation lights should have provided some warning of our approach.

Given that they didn't want to waste their precious battery power, the lights would only begin flashing when *Precious Metal* was virtually at their side. The yelling would continue until we had safely passed their local fishing territory and came upon the next screaming fisherman. Often they would lead us around their lines, which could be up to a kilometre long and point us in the right direction to avoid the next fisherman, but mostly we were left to fend for ourselves and re-establish our navigational heading. This pattern continued the entire night and was thoroughly exhausting. In order to avoid the seemingly endless array of fishermen, we decided to head further offshore another five to 10 miles. Much to our dismay we discovered even more insane fishermen the further out we went.

In our continuing state of fatigue, Barry and I decided to shorten our watches so that our manual steering regimen wasn't as exhausting. We had marginal success in tying the steering wheel into a constant straight position when the seas were flat which gave us some respite from being on the helm. Barry was extraordinarily understanding and patient, as this voyage was not an ideal experience. I compensated by letting him win our intensely competitive cribbage games! Thankfully, the window of weather that we experienced that week was calm and uneventful, although never sunny enough to activate the solar panels.

One exhausting day led into the next and before long we were approaching Salinas, Ecuador. I was able to phone ahead to reserve dock space and a wonderful (Canadian) mechanic named George was standing by to greet us on our arrival. Remarkably, as we rounded the point and headed into the harbour the red light on my battery meter began flashing – indicating that our batteries were in their final stages. I still recall George saying to Barry, "You should be thankful that your captain knows her boat so well or you'd be floating out to sea now and possibly never see land again!" This comment provided some marginal consolation for the arduous voyage we had finally and safely completed.

Dealing with the Ecuadorian Authorities

The urgency of requiring immediate electricity at the dock allowed us to enter Salinas under a special premise entitled 'State of Duress'. This is a nautical maritime provision that supersedes the traditional formalities of protocol for entering the country. At the time, I was confident that the authorities would be compassionate and understanding of our situation. What was I thinking? Instead, as it turned out, it caused us further grief with our entry procedures. Once the boat was secure at the dock, I was told by the marina manager that we could not disembark *Precious Metal* or have our mechanic board the boat until the following day in the late afternoon when all of the officials could be present to clear us for entry into the country.

One by one each official arrived for this meeting at *Precious Metal*: my required agent (who charged $300.00 for his services), the port captain, the agriculture representative, a customs person and a robust immigration gentleman. They all proceeded to sit around the main table in my salon as I offered them each a beverage. Most of them requested a soft drink, except for the immigration man was intent on drinking scotch. My initial impression was that each of these individuals was very gracious and personable. What was I thinking?

After his second scotch, the immigration representative brought the party to an abrupt halt when he announced that my clearance papers weren't executed correctly by the agent I hired in the Galapagos seven months earlier. A heated discussion ensued in rapid Spanish and I began to sense that I was in trouble. Finally they explained that because my paperwork was done incorrectly when I departed the Galapagos, I was theoretically still in Ecuador and had never departed. Since it was illegal to stay in the country for more than six months, I was therefore in the country illegally. Despite the fact that my passport showed travel to Peru, Mexico, United States, Canada and England since my departure from the Galapagos, they were intent on causing me grief.

They finally concluded that they could solve my situation by pretending that I wasn't in the country! My agent then discreetly mentioned that I should offer a bottle of scotch to the immigration official as a token of my appreciation for his cooperation.

At this point they took my passport and proceeded to remove my name from all of the forms, thereby making Barry the owner and captain of *Precious Metal*. I was absolutely livid. My paid agent from their own country had erred seven months earlier and I had no recourse but to accept their outrageous proposal. Was it possible that these male officials took exception to me being a female captain and found it culturally unacceptable? I will never know the answer.

I was also informed that I was not allowed to leave the marina except to buy essential provisions (and presumably more scotch) at the store a block away. Barry was free to wander at his will and I was essentially held captive with no passport until my boat was repaired and I could exit the country. My agent informed me that he would check in regularly to inquire about the boat repairs (and collect another bottle of scotch for his efforts as well as compensate the immigration officer for his extended complicity). He also assured me that my name would be reinstated on the paperwork upon my departure from Ecuador.

I'm confident that Ecuador is a wonderful country; however, my experience was truly horrifying. Barry found a wonderful gringo bar close to the marina and on two occasions during my 10 days of captivity we disguised my appearance and he whisked me off in a taxi for a fun evening. He also piggy-backed me to the theatre one night since I was refrained from walking the streets. Eventually George was able to import a new regulator from Florida and after 10 long days *Precious Metal* was once again ship-shape. I also had the back-up generator repaired by an elderly Ecuadorian man who sat cross-legged for an entire day on the dock, pulled the entire machine apart and put it back together.

On our final day in Salinas I contacted my agent and requested my passport as well as all the necessary documents required to leave Ecuador. In all, the cost of the marina, boat repairs, scotch and agent fees exceeded $2,300.00. After receiving my passport and all the paperwork I paid the marina bill and prepared *Precious Metal* for an early morning departure. Once my passport and documents were safely in my possession, I lectured my agent on his fiduciary responsibility as a representative of his country. I explained to him that if a boat arrived under duress into Canada, our authorities would have done everything in their power to assist. As my agent, his responsibility was to maintain the highest standards of professionalism and never succumb to bribery. I believe that I made him think seriously about his duty as an agent and hope I had some influence towards improving the experiences of future sailors in that region. Just after sunrise we cast off the dock and happily headed out of the bay. Our spirits were high.

Only 20 minutes had passed when suddenly a serious voice bellowed over the VHF, "*Precious Metal*, turn around and come back to the marina immediately." I barely had time to turn around before I saw a marina boat speeding towards us. With no explanation, the attending driver sternly insisted that I board his decrepit boat, leaving Barry to tend to *Precious Metal* and idle slowly around the bay. I quickly grabbed my purse and boat papers fearing the worst. I will never forget looking back as *Precious Metal* faded into the distance, watching Barry and my sweet little Riley standing helplessly on the stern with horrified looks of forlorn.

Upon my arrival at the marina one police boat was present as well as a formal line-up of official-looking men with stern faces. As I was ushered up the dock ramp and into the office, every marina attendant was staring at me with a look of impending doom. At this point I became terrified and imagined the horrid possibility of being sequestered in an Ecuadorian jail. I had absolutely no idea why I was being sought after nor my pending fate.

To my relief, the women in the office greeted me with their usual warm welcome in Spanish. I was handed a bill for $18.00 for an overnight charge for water and power which they had neglected to include on my bill the previous day. "All of this drama for $18.00?" I said. "No problemo!" I handed them a $20.00 bill and told them to keep the change. I didn't even wait for the receipt and within minutes I was back on the shuttle boat. Needless to say both Riley and Barry were delighted by my speedy return.

Our sails were hoisted immediately as we motored out of the bay. We used every form of propulsion to exit out of Ecuadorian waters as quickly as possible for fear that another drama would surface. I'm confident that Ecuador has many terrific highlights to explore, but I could not get out of the country fast enough.

CHAPTER 12

Central America: An Electrifying Experience

December 2010

My Ecuadorian nightmare put me behind schedule by nearly two weeks, so I decided to bypass Panama and head straight to Golfito, Costa Rica, from Salinas. The atmosphere aboard *Precious Metal* was euphoric during this section of the voyage given that all of our systems were once again functioning perfectly. The week-long passage was one big party with music blaring, fishing lines in the water, delicious feasts each evening and highly competitive card games (which I continued to lose). What was I thinking? I now believe that Barry was a professional card player in another life as I barely won a game and owed him over $50.00 in lost bets by the end of the voyage.

Our arrival at Golfito was a pleasant surprise. Golfito is located in a stunningly beautiful natural harbour with several hospitable pubs along the shoreline creating a festive atmosphere for visitors and locals. I fell in love with this tiny community which became my base for extended periods of time over the course of the following two years. My special friends Katie and Tim have owned and operated a cruiser-friendly business called Land and Sea and have provided a cruisers' 'home away from home' environment for over 20 years.

It sounds crazy, but for the following two years I transited the region between Zihuatanejo, Mexico, and Panama five times for a variety of reasons that are discussed in future chapters. My first priority was to return to Zihuatanejo to coordinate Sail Fest again which was my pet project and seemed to justify my otherwise self-indulgent lifestyle. The 1,000-mile stretch between Golfito and southern Mexico can be challenging due to two notable weather systems: the Papagayo (southern Nicaragua) and Tehuantepec (southern Mexico) winds which develop in the Gulf of Mexico on the Caribbean side of Central America and funnel through the steep valleys. Occasionally these weather systems have created sudden hurricane force winds along the Pacific coast. Prudent sailors have often waited weeks for a safe passage across these regions.

Instead of following the coast line and being subjected to weather delays, I decided to take a more exciting offshore route and sail to the remote Cocos Islands which are owned by Costa Rica and have a wonderful reputation for exotic marine and bird life – most notably the infamous hammerhead shark. These unique islands were only accessible by boat and were managed by a team of young volunteer rangers.

My friend Michael Savino from Denver, Colorado, was keen to join me on this voyage given that he was a master scuba diver and experienced sailor. Michael and I met many years ago while sailing on separate boats in the Caribbean and re-united on Facebook. He was recently part of our delightful group that ventured down the Amazon River in Peru.

We departed Golifto on December 19 in order to arrive at the Cocos Islands just in time for Christmas. I phoned the Cocos Islands ranger station ahead of our departure to see if they needed any supplies. Their only request was for light bulbs. We prepared a wonderful bounteous Christmas basket full of tasty food items as well as lots of light bulbs, which these isolated volunteers truly appreciated.

Our voyage to the Cocos Islands was uneventful although much slower than anticipated due to strong adverse currents and headwinds during the majority of the three-day passage. Sighting the initial outline of land on the horizon brought cheers of joy and excitement knowing that very few people ever have had an opportunity to explore these magnificent tropical islands.

Adjectives cannot describe the breath-taking beauty of these islands as we approached the protected bay that became our home for the following three nights. Lush green mountainous outcrops were surrounded by crystal clear blue water and brilliant white sandy beaches that circled our bay. Thousands of young white fluffy booby birds were nesting in the trees. Mother Nature was at her very best when she created these incredibly beautiful islands. Furthermore, we had them all to ourselves and were completely alone with not a soul or another boat in sight.

We hailed the ranger station on the VHF and were instructed to attach our boat to one of the mooring buoys provided for visiting boats. (Anchoring is prohibited in this marine park in order to protect the marine habitats on the ocean floor.) Before long we were greeted by a group of rangers in a rudimentary fishing boat and processed the necessary paperwork that allowed us to stay for three days. These amicable young rangers proudly described the special features of the islands and offered to take us on an inland hike to a picturesque waterfall the following day. We were encouraged to snorkel and Michael was able to arrange a day of scuba diving. Our three days at the Cocos Islands were filled with lots of activity in this beautiful natural playground while we enjoyed the warm hospitality of the rangers.

The timing of this voyage was fortuitous insofar as we were able to observe these pristine islands before any development had taken place. Other than a few ranger dormitories and cooking facilities that were unobtrusively constructed and strategically hidden inland, there was absolutely no sign of human existence. We snorkelled for hours along the coastline discovering many species of rare tropical fish and never encountered a piece of garbage on the shores or ocean floor. The water was so clear that we had visibility several fathoms deep and spent hours mesmerized by the abundance of fish swimming directly below the boat. Michael was overjoyed when he returned from his scuba diving excursion and repeatedly said that it was his best scuba experience ever. Sadly, I understand that in the two years since my visit, a tourist centre has now been erected and cruisers can no longer visit without extensive preliminary paperwork and exorbitant nightly fees.

We departed the Cocos Islands on Christmas Day morning after a sumptuous breakfast feast. The seas were flat with not a breath of wind. Suddenly, a giant great blue whale rose within 100 feet of *Precious Metal*'s bow. My first reaction was that it was a rogue wave coming from out of nowhere because it extended a tremendous distance perpendicular to the boat. Then I thought it must be several whales because of the size. Finally, I realized that it was one magnificent blue whale – which was an extraordinary sight against the flat calm seas. I accepted this as Mother Nature's Christmas present and one that I will cherish and remember my entire life.

After the spectacular whale sighting, our voyage to Zihuatanejo was relatively uneventful. We made a short stop for a few days in Huatulco, Mexico, to check into the country and celebrate traditional New Year's festivities.

I decided to remain in the community of Zihuatanejo for several months to help coordinate Sail Fest and attend their annual Guitar Fest. Both events were tremendous successes. If I didn't need to take *Precious Metal* somewhere safe for hurricane season (May through October) I could easily have made Zihuatanejo my home. All good things must come to an end and by mid-March it was time to move on.

My former crew member Jim and another high-spirited young man named Leo joined *Precious Metal* during the next passage back to Golfito, Costa Rico. Leo was a fabulous French chef and prepared incredibly delicious meals including morning chocolate crepes which were his signature dish. Jim continued to entertain us with his lively humour and we managed to find ample wind in both the Tehuatepec and Papagayo regions for some terrific sailing. Our only major stop-over was in Bahia del

Sol, El Salvador, where we took part in several days of the annual El Salvador Cruiser's Rally that offers some terrific local activities for sailors.

To my pleasant surprise I discovered that El Salvador was a hospitable and picturesque developing country with beautiful long stretches of virgin beaches. I also realized that the anchorage in Bahia del Sol was an ideal place to store my boat during hurricane season as it was well protected and inexpensive. For once, saying good-bye wasn't too difficult because I was reasonably confident that I would be returning soon. Little did I know at the time that I would be returning less than two months later and under extremely dire circumstances

To Costa Rica and Back

Cruisers have often referred to their itineraries as being cast in Jello or written in sand at low tide. Our nomadic cruising lifestyle is unique because our floating home allows us to travel to any place in the world that is by an ocean. Other than weather constraints, places that are associated with danger, costs and each respective country's visa protocol, the cruising sailor has unlimited freedom to decide future plans and destinations. After having been so impressed with El Salvador during my short five-day stay, I realized that it made much more sense to return the Bahia del Sol than continue on to Panama for hurricane season.

Accordingly, shortly after my departure from Bahia del Sol, I decided to abandon my short-term plans for Panama. I would continue sailing another 600 miles to Golfito with Jim and Leo, enjoy Costa Rica for a month and return to El Salvador to catch the end of the El Salvador Cruiser's Rally on May 1. My friend Michael agreed to fly to Golfito and join me on my return voyage to Bahia del Sol since he had never been to this region of Central America. We departed Golfito early morning on April 20 on a seemingly routine voyage that would ultimately change my life for the following 18 months.

Lightning Strikes Precious Metal

I confess to being a little blasé about the return 600-mile voyage to El Salvador, having just covered the same stretch of ocean the month before. Furthermore, Michael was a highly capable sailor and savvy with mechanical and electrical systems so I could rely on him if *Precious Metal* needed repairs. What was I thinking? In hindsight, I was probably becoming a little too confident and perhaps slightly cavalier with regards to ocean passages – a weakness that Mother Nature decided to correct one evening 400 miles into our voyage.

We were 35 nautical miles off the coast of Nicaragua and 200 miles from our destination of Bahia del Sol. It was 8.00pm and Michael had just gone to bed while I stayed on deck for my three hour watch. The sky was dark with the exception of mesmerizing bolts of electricity from an intense lightning storm in the distance. I remember sitting comfortably in my cockpit privately commending Mother Nature for her remarkable fireworks show. During my routine boat inspection when I checked the gauges on the instrument panel, horizon, engine room and walked around the decks, I noted on my radar that the lightning cells were a safe 20 miles away and therefore I had no need to worry.

My first clue that something was amiss was the sudden arrival of birds surrounding *Precious Metal*. A huge flock of tiny petrels seemed to appear from nowhere and began swarming the boat. Several flew inside while at least 50 landed on the deck and seemed to be semi-comatose. I quickly managed to grab Riley's dog cage and capture the birds that flew inside the boat, using a towel as a net. By this time, Michael appeared from his cabin and helped me gather the remaining few birds. As I climbed up the companionway to release the birds from the cage I noticed that my emergency light on the dash was lit. Seeing this light sent a clear signal to me that something was gravely wrong and I immediately shut down the engine.

Suddenly I smelled smoke. After quickly dashing through the cabins it was apparent that the smoke was coming from the engine room. We had a quick discussion of whether I should release the engine room's Halon fire extinguisher (which is accessed under the companionway stairs). I was reluctant to make this decision until we had properly assessed the gravity of the situation. In hindsight we made the right decision because of the incompatibility of the type of fire we were dealing with and the chemicals that this type of extinguisher emits. We chose not to open the engine room door and provide more oxygen to the fire. Instead, I slowly lifted the small trap door in the main salon floor and dark black smoke immediately came billowing out. At this stage we could assume that the smoke was not from a flaming fire and was probably due to an electrical or mechanical problem.

After several minutes I was able to clear out enough of the smoke to descend into the engine room through the trap door using a flashlight for visibility. I instantly noticed that one of the main wiring bundles mounted on the roof of the engine room had somehow come loose and fallen onto the hot engine block. My first reaction was that this was the cause of the smoke and proceeded to move the bundle off the engine and secure it to an adjacent hose with a temporary strap. It was still too smoky to see around the rest of the engine compartment.

Several minutes later the smoke began to clear and I directed my flashlight around the room. My heart sank. "Oh my God!" I exclaimed, trying to contain myself and digest the scope of the damage around me. I simply sat there in awe. Every single bundle of wiring was fried, black and hanging loosely by melted strapping. The walls of the engine room were scorched in every area along the course of the wiring. The smell of melted plastic wiring insulation was sickening. The scene around me was daunting. Michael tried to call for assistance on the VHF radio but it was no longer functioning. He then attempted to call on our hand-held VHF radio but no other boat was in close enough range to hear our call.

At this stage we had not concluded that lightning was the cause, but after Michael assessed the situation it was clear that we had had a severe electrical fire throughout the engine room. We systematically tried to evaluate which systems were still

Lightning struck Precious Metal's *entire wiring system,*
frying every bundle of wire in the boat

functioning on the boat. Fortunately the engine and wiring to the batteries and alternators were intact so we were able to use the motor. We had no cabin or navigation lights and the pump that drives the autopilot was damaged so we were faced with having to hand-steer. The radar was also compromised, as well as the GPS – the instrument that gives our position. Fortunately, I had a hand-held GPS that allowed us to navigate. Knowing that there was potential for further electrical shorting made us realize that we immediately needed to begin cutting all of the wiring in the engine room. I grabbed the wire cutters from the tool kit and proceeded to cut every wire in the bundles that were damaged.

It took nearly two hours to sever all the wiring in the engine room. During this time, Michael stood watch in the cockpit and operated the boat. I could only work in short spurts because I felt nauseous from the chemical fumes and smoke. At times I felt dizzy but I had to persevere or we faced the possibility of another fire. At one stage during the two hours I poured myself a bath to relax and settle my nerves which seemed to help. By 11.00pm that evening I was confident that all the wiring was disengaged from the electronics and respective power sources. Mishaps on a boat always seem to be magnified at night and while we both managed to remain calm, the atmosphere aboard was subdued. It was a very long night.

We alternated our watches on a need-to-sleep basis and manually steered until daylight with only our hand-held GPS and compass as our guide. I considered altering course and heading into Nicaragua which was only half a day away. However, after a lot of thought and discussion we decided to proceed to our original destination, Bahia del Sol, another 200 miles away. My reasoning was that I knew that whatever port I went to would be my home for a very long time to get everything repaired. I was not familiar with the trades and services along the northern coast of Nicaragua, but I knew there would be excellent support and services in Bahia del Sol. It was a time when I needed to be with my friends and I also knew many of the cruisers in Bahia del Sol were capable of assisting with my repairs.

As I was cooking a hearty breakfast early the following morning I once again smelled smoke. Electrical smoke has a unique and horrid smell from the chemicals and wire insulation. Once breakfast was finished Michael said that while I was in the galley cooking breakfast he too smelled smoke and discovered another run of shorted wiring in the electrical panel that leads to the electronics in the cockpit. He didn't want to upset me with this news until after breakfast when we solemnly and reluctantly were forced to cut all of the wiring to the main dashboard and instrument panel.

The tension aboard was finally dispelled around mid-morning when I suddenly realized, "The birds!" In all of the drama the previous evening I forgot to release the birds from Riley's cage! What was I thinking? I raced to the back deck and grabbed the cage. Inside were four tiny petrel birds cuddled together beneath the towel with their wide eyes peering at me suspiciously. I carefully released them from the cage and set them free. What were they thinking during their 14 hours of captivity?

The following 36 hours were some of the longest in my

life. My precious boat had been totally compromised and it took everything I had to stay positive. I was confident that my insurance would cover the repairs, but until I did a full assessment of the damage when I arrived into port I could barely look into the engine room without getting pangs of extreme sadness. We came to the conclusion that the lightning storm that night had caused the damage – even from a distance of 20 miles.

The entrance into Bahia del Sol can be extremely stressful due to a huge moving sand bar that stretches across the opening to the marina and anchorage. Boats are required to anchor outside the entrance until high slack tide which means that one can only enter the bay once a day. The government provides a pilot named Rohileo to safely usher boats across the bar on his skidoo and guide them into the anchorage.

We arrived at the entrance coordinates in time for high tide on April 30 and Rohileo greeted us with his wonderful warm smile. After a great sleigh ride across the bar I steered *Precious Metal* into the marina dock. Many of my wonderful cruising friends were waiting to take our lines and help secure the boat.

Crossing the bar into Bahia del Sol, El Salvador. Another electrifying experience!

Bill and Jean of the boat *Mita Kuuluu* are the organizers of the El Salvador Rally and gave us a warm welcome. Finally, *Precious Metal* was secure and we felt relieved that we had survived our lightning strike safely.

I have learned a lot about lightning since this incident. *Precious Metal*'s rare encounter with lightning was referred to as 'a bolt out of the blue'. These bolts of lightning occur in the middle of the ocean and when they hit the water they need to find something to ground them in order to dissipate. As they search for grounding they gain speed, momentum and force. It's believed that the birds were exposed to the electromagnetic force of the lightning and sought *Precious Metal* for safety.

My surveyor concluded that the bolt entered *Precious Metal* through the exhaust and swept through the engine room before dissipating through the keel. It is also believed that *Precious Metal*'s steel hull saved us because the power of the bolt was so enormous that an aluminium or wooden hull could have caught on fire, while lightning to a fibreglass hull is sometimes causes blown-through hulls due to the extreme forces of electricity.

I have also come to the conclusion that lightning has a mind of its own and nothing could have prevented this strike. There are many theories surrounding lightning and the precautions to prevent a strike; however, after endless discussions and research, my theory is that lightning will do whatever it wants. I was simply in the wrong place at the wrong time. Another possibility is that Mother Nature recognized that my skills and knowledge regarding electrical systems were weak. Perhaps she was thinking: "I'll teach her how to handle electrical systems and zap her with some lightning! Then she'll have to become proficient in electrical skills."

Every unfortunate situation has a silver lining. For the following seven months I was forced to re-wire my entire boat (with the assistance of many people) and can happily report that I've mastered the one system of my boat that I had avoided and feared the most: electrical repairs and maintenance.

CHAPTER 13

Central America to Panama

May 2011

THE AFTERMATH OF *Precious Metal's* lightning strike was a long, frustrating and arduous process: mentally, physically and medically speaking. I was easily distracted from the lightning event during my first two weeks in Bahia del Sol because of the activity surrounding the El Salvador Cruiser's Rally and my wonderful friends in the bay. We arrived in port on the day of the Grand Finale party for the Cruiser's Rally where I danced the night away catching up with so many supportive cruising friends who had recently arrived from Mexico.

Michael departed the following day and my special friend Joanne arrived so I was never without great company. That said, it took weeks to recover mentally from the lightning strike and the resulting damage. The scarred burnt walls around *Precious Metal's* engine room, the lingering smell of putrid smoke and the inability to use most of *Precious Metal's* electrical and mechanical systems were constant reminders of the tragedy. I chose to sleep on board *Precious Metal* at the dock during the following nights because I wanted to be close by in case of another electrical shorting.

My first priority was to report the lightning incident to my insurance company and file a comprehensive claim. I could not have asked for a more professional and compassionate response from my insurer. Craig Chamberlain at Mariner's Insurance responded to my claim immediately by writing, "Pamela, we are truly sorry for this occurrence and we will ensure that *Precious Metal* will be restored to her original sea shape condition as quickly and as painlessly as possible." I'm pleased to report that Mariner's Insurance did not let me down. Fortunately, my policy allowed for electrical repairs from lightning with a small deductible and the payment to repair the damage was in my bank account within six weeks.

A small annoying sore began to develop on my elbow shortly after my arrival into Bahia del Sol. Thinking that it was a minor spider bite, I paid little attention to it at first. Gradually, over the course of several days, more sores appeared and soon my entire torso was covered in a rare outbreak of lesions. It appeared that I had something similar to chicken pox although there was no associated pain or itchiness. At the same time, I also noticed that my limbs were becoming numb. I had virtually no feeling in my hands or feet and very little in my legs and arms.

Finally, after attempting to apply various medical topical remedies to the lesions without any noticeable improvement, I was persuaded by several nurses in the cruising fleet to seek medical attention. After many tests and visits to the internal medicine specialist whom I was referred to in San Salvador, Dr Ernesto concluded that I endured severe toxin exposure from the chemicals in the fried wiring and my immune system had been compromised. What was I thinking? I should never have entered the smoky engine room without a face mask.

There's a temptation to doubt the competence of medical professionals in developing countries and I admit to questioning whether I should return to Canada for a 'proper' opinion. My doubts were completely cast aside on my first appointment with Dr Ernesto. The initial consultation took over an hour and I was totally impressed by his thoroughness. My weekly follow-up appointments to ensure that the medications prescribed were appropriate were reassuring. On one occasion he suggested I return in five days and then said, "Instead of coming to my office, I would like my wife to meet you. Please come to our home for coffee next Sunday!" He and his wife were gracious hosts and after our delightful visit I was driven back to *Precious Metal* with my arms full of fresh coconuts to share with my cruising buddies.

During Joanne's two-week visit, we joined four of my favourite cruising couples and hired Jorge Martinez, a local travel agent, to take us on an eight-day inland tour of Honduras, Central Guatemala and Tikal – a World Heritage Site in the northern, historical Mayan region of Guatemala. We all had a terrific time enjoying interesting sites, great camaraderie and tons of laughter. Surprisingly, there are a number of fabulous high-end hotels strategically nestled in these remote developing regions.

Jorge was a tremendous ambassador for his country and incredibly knowledgeable with regard to the history and local facts. On our final drive back to Bahia del Sol the group sang a humorous song for Jorge that we had created – dedicated to the obvious pride he had for his country. Tears streamed down his cheeks as we sang aloud in the bus. Sadly, this tour would be one of his last. Jorge died of a massive heart attack several months later while he was promoting El Salvador at a trade show in Columbia. Our hearts will remain with Jorge, his devoted wife Morena and young son Jorge (Jr) forever.

A fellow cruiser in the bay (John aboard the M/V *Sea Quest*) was competent in boat repairs and had assisted me on several occasions while I was in Mexico several years prior. I hired him to do the preliminary rewiring while I flew back to Canada to select new electronic equipment. It took John six weeks of gruelling work to completely re-wire the boat in the hot, humid climate. Finally, upon my return from Canada late July I was able to move off the dock into an anchorage where I am always much happier.

A cute, young El Salvadorian man named Santos approached *Precious Metal* almost immediately after I secured the boat on my designated mooring buoy. Santos welcomed me into the bay and advised me that he had a boat maintenance and repair business. He explained that his company was well qualified and could do every kind of boat repair imaginable as well as provide maintenance services. "Perfect!" I replied. "I need someone to clean my engine room. It's filthy from the electrical fire and re-wiring work." Santos agreed and scheduled an early morning start the following day. His fee was $20.00 per day.

Santos and his co-worker Samuel worked in the engine room for most of the day. I could hear them whistling and laughing aloud as I performed topside duties. Finally, at around 4.00pm they surfaced stating that the job was complete. I descended into the engine room to inspect the work that was done and discovered that the room was still filthy.

"Santos, it's still really dirty," I exclaimed. I showed him how filthy the floor was and ran my fingers along the walls indicating that the charred areas that still needed to be cleaned. He agreed to return the following day. "We always want you to be happy with our work," he said. At the end of the following day, after providing more cleaning cloths and detergent, the engine room still showed little to no improvement. What were they doing down there for so many hours?

What was I thinking? A day later I was walking by Santos' home on the shore of the bay and suddenly realized why there was so little improvement in my engine room. These families live in shacks with dirt floors, virtually no walls and a make-shift corrugated roof. There's nothing to clean! How could they possibly know about cleaning when they live in such crude structures? It occurred to me that they might have wondered whether they should sprinkle a load of dirt on the engine room floor!

There's a reason why Santos and other local entrepreneurs in Bahia del Sol only charge $20.00 per day. The realization of how basic their lives are made me understand the huge discrepancy between their version of a boat maintenance versus my expectations as well as other future cruisers who would be hiring him. Knowing that rudimentary tasks such as cleaning was foreign to Santos, I called him back to my boat the following day and explained the various cleaning techniques for each area of a boat. He was keen to get started again and by the end of the day my engine room was sparkling clean.

For the balance of the following three months in Bahia

del Sol, other cruisers and I employed Santos and a number of other locals to assist in boat repairs and maintenance. Santos's business began to expand and he was able to hire and train many of his friends and relatives. I did notice, however, that his administrative skills were lacking. He wasn't keeping track of his costs, receipts or lists of duties that he had promised to fulfil on the various boats. I provided him with a leather-bound portfolio with sheets of papers for notes, a section for business cards and a spreadsheet for his finances. He gratefully thanked me and replied, "Now I feel like a businessman. But a businessman needs shoes." The following day he and his fellow workers all came to work wearing shoes. It takes so little to help these wonderful people who are so incredibly appreciative.

One day I had to go to San Salvador to have some cushions re-upholstered. Santos graciously offered to drive since he also needed some supplies. What was I thinking? We departed in Santos' decrepit old half-ton truck promptly at 9.00am with two other cruising friends on what would normally be a 90-minute drive. I was squished in the middle of the front seat with my friend Henry beside me as we travelled along the dirt road at a painfully slow speed. None of Santos' dash gauges worked so I had no idea of how slow we were going. Several bicycles passed us along the way as well as some horses doing a slow trot. Suddenly, Santos pulled over to the side of the road and stopped the truck. He jumped out and quickly raised the hood. Apparently he had forgotten to put oil in the engine. "No problem," he said. "I have lots of oil for the rest of the trip."

A short time later, we heard a strange sound from under the hood. "No problem," he said. "The radiator breaks loose sometimes. I have a friend that can help." A mile or so later we pulled into a driveway and his friend helped him lift and secure the radiator with rope through the grill. As we were watching this repair, my friend Henry noticed the tires and said to Santos, "Santos, do you think your tires are a little low on air?" "No problem," said Santos. "I have a friend." Needless to say, after another few miles we pulled into another friend's driveway and put air in the tires. At this point, it was 11.00am and we still hadn't left the dirt road that led to the main highway!

The truck limped along the highway hugging the right shoulder while vehicles whizzed past us for the balance of the journey. We finally arrived in San Salvador at 1.00pm, hot and hungry. Our errands in the city were somewhat stressful because the list of tasks was long and we needed to be back in Bahia del Sol before dark since the truck had no headlights. "I have lights but they don't shine," he said with a serious look.

Sure enough, our departure from San Salvador was after sunset which meant driving back to the anchorage at even slower speeds in the dark on the far right shoulder with vehicles seemingly passing us at Mach speed. During this arduous trip back, all I could think of was François – my limousine driver during my past career in the investment business, wondering if I ever told him how truly I appreciated him?

A lovely young man named Hector approached me one day saying that he was a wood-worker and built furniture. I decided that this could be a great opportunity to have a new table built for my cockpit. Hector spoke no English. Henry and I were beginning to spend a lot of time together and he helped me design a table that had a removable leaf on one side and was measured to fit perfectly in the cockpit. Hector listened intently as I explained (in Spanish) the diagram with size and dimensions and assured me that he would deliver my table in one week. What was I thinking?

Exactly one week later Hector and his young friend arrived at my boat in his dugout canoe with a table that would fit a full size dining room. They had paddled two miles up the river from his home with this gigantic piece of furniture – a table that I could never even load onto the boat – let alone fit in the cockpit. "Mucho, mucho grande!" I exclaimed. "Where is the paper with the measurements?" Hector shook his head. I could tell that he was so disheartened because I wasn't overjoyed with his masterpiece. I felt so badly. He explained that the paper was at his house and asked me to come to his house the following day.

Finding Hector's home was another story. I invited my friend and fellow cruiser Shannon (who speaks excellent Spanish) to join me on this excursion that required us to dinghy two miles up a winding river to the town of Herradura – a small community which reminded me of scenes from the movie *Deliverance*. Upon arrival, we were directed to a building where his friend would join us and lead us to his house. We walked for another 10 minutes along a crude dirt path past shacks and families living in absolute, abject, unimaginable poverty.

Finally we arrived at Hector's home and workshop. Only then did I realize that he didn't own a measuring tape. How could he have interpreted the measurements? What was I thinking? It broke my heart knowing that he tried so hard to build a beautiful table based on his own perceptions of design and measurements. Furthermore, hauling it through the town and up the river to my boat and then back again must have made him think that he had failed – especially in the eyes of his family and village.

It took one more visit to Hector's home to teach him how to measure and finish the table. Henry also spent a full day demonstrating and teaching Hector how to fill and finish the wood. Sadly, Hector didn't know that wood needs to be dried before construction – particularly wood from humid regions. My new table weighed about 100 pounds and has slowly been drying out in several pieces around the boat in order to stay flat. With any luck I will be able to use it in five years – that's if it doesn't warp or crack!

One day a handful of cruisers were invited to attend a meeting in San Salvador that was hosted by the government in an effort to understand how the country could further develop nautical tourism. I was very impressed by the people at the highest levels of El Salvadorian government. The boardroom was comprised of representatives from, among others: the Departments of Tourism, heads of the Navy, Customs and Immigration.

Many of these savvy government officials were refugees during the Civil War and had been educated in the United States. They spoke fluent English and were highly progressive in

The arrival of Hector's masterpiece cockpit table by panga

their thinking in terms of improving the health and economy of their country. Unlike many developing countries, they were fully aware of the benefits that cruisers bring to their country.

Contrary to traditional tourists, cruisers generally stay in the country for longer periods and spend more money across every level of society – grocery and hardware stores, mechanical services and electronic stores as well as having time for inland travel and eating in the local restaurants. They were fascinated by our comments and recommendations and understood our need for security, easy entrance and exit protocol, visa requirements and so on. Their current support for the El Salvador Cruiser's Rally is a testimony to their strong commitment.

Towards the end of the meeting I discussed the need to address garbage. "Tourists are offended by garbage and it's everywhere – particularly along every beach," I explained. "Not only is it offensive, but the El Salvadorian people need to be educated that garbage and poor sanitation is extremely harmful to their environment and health." They all nodded their heads in agreement and then one woman spoke.

She told us about a garbage campaign that they had launched the previous year where a certain section of beachfront had been designated as the pilot project. All the local residents were encouraged to volunteer the entire day cleaning up the beach garbage. At the end of the day, officials had a big surprise when they came by to pick up the garbage. They found palm boughs, coconuts and dead natural materials piled up, while the plastic debris and man-made garbage was still left on the beach!

The campaign was re-enacted the following week but this time the officials explained to the volunteers the meaning of garbage. They also supplied recycling bins to separate the different types of garbage. The resident volunteers learned that plastics, shoes and man-made items constitute garbage and need to be picked up off the beach. Once again, the volunteers began working tirelessly to collect and separate the various garbage items into their respective bins. The officials were impressed with their work and decided to reward the volunteers. A truck load of snacks arrived as a token of gratitude for their hard work. Sadly, the snacks were packaged in Styrofoam wrapping and plastic juice containers which were soon strewn all over their nicely manicured beach! Everyone at the meeting agreed that education is the crux of so many environmental issues in developing countries.

By the end of August all of my repairs were completed except the autopilot – which is critical for single-handed sailing.

The local Garmin distributor, Gabriel, who owns a marine store called Marinsa assured me that he had ordered the correct model according to my boat's specifications and photographs. I hired a qualified electrician and fellow cruiser named Tim to help me install my new autopilot and after a month of frustration we still could not get it to function properly.

Despite many attempts to convince Gabriel to honour Garmin's good reputation and investigate the problem, he insisted that I hire his own mechanic for far too much money and with the proviso that neither Tim nor I be present when his mechanic does the work. I became very suspicious of Gabriel's work ethic and decided that my only recourse was to hand-steer over 1,000 miles to Panama where I hoped to find a reputable Garmin dealer. It took over a year and endless hours of gruelling fatigue from manual steering to and throughout Panama to finally determine that my suspicions about Gabriel were correct.*

Introducing Henry

During the course of my summer in Bahia del Sol, I developed a relationship with a single-hander from California named Henry Robinson aboard his 42-foot catamaran *Rapscullion*. Henry had been sailing for over eight years and seemed to have a unique approach to the cruising lifestyle. My first impressions were that he was extremely laid back and loved being at one with Mother Nature.

While the majority of my days were spent working on *Precious Metal*'s repairs, Henry and I always found time in the late afternoons to body surf in the ocean and walk the beaches collecting shells. Another plus was that Riley was enamoured with Henry's willingness to include him on our excursions. Being the only solo sailors in the bay allowed us both to have a meaningful companionship with another solo cruiser.

Fish and chicken became our stable diet throughout Central America. One day early in the summer, Henry and I wandered down the road to a 'fish' restaurant that was recommended. It

The conclusion to this autopilot story takes place a year later in Panama, in Chapter 14.

turned out to be a picnic table outside a family home (shack) with cows, dogs and chickens running throughout the grounds. When the gracious owner asked what we wanted to eat we both replied, "Fish." "No fish today," she said. "Just chicken." "Okay, then I guess we'll have chicken," we replied. She pointed to the fowl running around under our feet asking, "Which one?" After a lot of consideration I chose the one that looked the least similar to the others in an effort to not break up any family. At least we were confident that it was fresh!

Henry's birthday falls on September 1 and by this time I needed a break from boat work. I decided to rent a car for his birthday and drive inland for a few days to the region surrounding the town of Suchitoto. We stayed in a lovely hotel and had such a wonderful time that we extended our trip another five days. Prior to our departure, I had researched possible destinations for our journey and was disillusioned by the negative warnings posted on various travel sites regarding crime towards tourists in El Salvador. In particular, the United States Travel Advisory is the most scathing and misleading. We travelled into so many wonderful communities where we were always treated like royalty.

On one occasion we ventured off the highway into a tiny village and as we parked the vehicle a man came running up the street exclaiming, "Are you a tourist?"

"Yes, I guess so," we replied curiously.

"I'm the tourist representative for this town and you're my first customer!" he said with excitement. He introduced himself as Poncho and proceeded to lead us to his tiny tourist booth. This darling young man had prepared comprehensive pamphlets that explained the history and local highlights of the surrounding area. We joined Poncho on a delightful tour of the church and local artisan shops. This kind of reception was exemplary of what took place in virtually every community we visited. It's tragic and unjust that a country of such genuinely caring people could be so grossly misrepresented by international tourism agencies and the media.

Henry was particularly attentive towards my medical issues and continuously monitored my sores to ensure they were healing. He also cooked me dinner each night after long days of wiring repairs on *Precious Metal*. My arms and legs were slowly but gradually regaining their feeling. By the end of September we decided to buddy boat to Panama, along with two other boats, whose owners had also become great friends: *Dragon's Toy* (Tom and Carrie) and *Sweetie* (Shannon and Tony). This decision to buddy boat with Henry was quite monumental for me, because it would be my first true experience as a single-hander. Until this time, I had always invited other people aboard for extended ocean passages.

While I've been incredibly fortunate to have enjoyed the company of many guests during my ocean voyages, it was becoming apparent to me that single-handing offered a simpler option in the more remote regions. People would book their flights a long time in advance which meant that my itinerary was no longer flexible. It's almost impossible to guarantee the arrival and departure date at future locations for a boat because boat repairs and maintenance, weather hazards and so many other factors play significant roles in operating the boat and impact the duration of voyage. I finally felt comfortable being a solo sailor on *Precious Metal* knowing that a competent fellow sailor would be nearby in case I needed assistance. What was I thinking?

My departure from Bahia del Sol was bitter-sweet. While I was anxious to finally head out to sea and explore new destinations, the friends I made in Bahia del Sol were incredibly supportive and had successfully brought me through an otherwise horrific period. We bid our final farewells to Santos and all of our local friends at a final gathering on October 6, with our boats fully provisioned for an extended time at sea.

After successfully crossing Bahia del Sol's sand bar, *Rapscullion* and *Precious Metal* sailed within sight of each other until darkness and found a reasonable anchoring location at sunset – about a mile off the coast in open water (also referred to as a roadstead anchorage). Our boats pitched and rolled all night but by sunrise the seas had calmed. The following afternoon we caught up with our friends (who had sailed overnight) at our first pristine anchorage off Manguera Island in the Gulf of Fonseca.

No sooner had we secured our anchors when our friends advised us that an intense tropical storm (Tropical Storm 12E) was on our path and would be upon us the following afternoon. Our only recourse for protection was to head 12 miles up Honduras's San Lorenzo Channel to the remote town of San Lorenzo where very few sailboats venture. Without delay, our four boats weighed anchor early the following morning and we carefully navigated our way up the narrow, mangrove-lined channel.

While the channel was surprisingly well marked with buoys I felt like an early explorer motoring so far into the hinterlands of Honduras. The channel became very narrow and increasingly shallow as we navigated close to the town of San Lorenzo, ultimately forcing us to use our hand-held depth sounders in our dinghies to safely find our way into the bay. Upon our arrival it became evident that this town receives very few visiting boats because the bay was lined with curious local onlookers observing our boats landing in our new anchorage.

The rule of thumb when a boat first enters a country is to report to customs and immigration officials. We took our dinghies into a make-shift dock at the far edge of the anchorage and much to our surprise, both officials were waiting for us. They greeted each of us with a welcoming handshake and introduced themselves. Then one officer took command in his broken English.

"Today is Friday and this is a holiday long-weekend. We would like you to check in next Tuesday," he said.

"We plan to depart after the storm leaves which will probably be next Wednesday," we explained.

"No problemo," he said. "We will check you in on Tuesday and out on Wednesday. Please be at our Customs office at 3.00pm next Tuesday."

We all laughed, given that most country officials take their jobs much more seriously and would never allow us to remain in their country for four days without extensive protocol.

San Lorenzo was surprisingly pleasant and overwhelmingly hospitable to us. Being the only Honduran tourist town on the Pacific coast, it was reasonably clean, safe and offered several upscale restaurants. People would stop their cars in the middle of the street just to speak with us and practice their English. As the tropical storm blew furiously 12 miles out at sea our wonderful refuge was truly delightful.

The numbness continued in my arms and legs and was becoming increasingly painful due to nerve damage from lightning. Henry and I decided to seek medical attention and a local restaurateur provided the name of a reputable doctor. The clinic was basic but clean. It was apparent that I needed another series of injections which meant that Henry would need to learn how to administer the needles. The doctor was very patient in describing the proper technique to Henry, although we both hated needles and dreaded the thought of him giving me my injection. After two visits to the clinic my condition improved substantially and thankfully we were able to make it to the next port without Henry having to play nurse. To my surprise, my doctor's visit in Honduras cost $3.00 – 50 cents for the doctor; 50 cents for the needle and $2.00 for the medication.

One morning I was running my engine to charge the batteries and doing some light interior boat cleaning. Suddenly, I heard what sounded like gunshots outside in the distance, although initially I was too preoccupied to pay much attention. The shots continued so I finally peered outside the boat. A man was on his balcony shooting his handgun over the bay. "He must be shooting birds," I thought and proceeded with my chores. The shots didn't stop. I looked again and he had apparently switched the handgun for a large rifle.

People were beginning to congregate along the shore so I finally took some interest. As I climbed into the cockpit it became clear that he was shooting in my direction and screaming at me! "What's all the commotion about?" I screamed, wondering if I should wave a white flag? Finally, in his broken English he advised me that my boat was leaking fuel into the water. I discovered that a fuel hose had fallen off the engine causing diesel to enter into the bilge and be pumped out into the bay. Only in Honduras do they use such extreme measures to attract attention!

The six of us congregated in the Customs office at exactly 3.00pm on the following Tuesday. Despite the custom official's four-day notice, he had no idea what do with us or which papers to complete. He began phoning several different agencies for information. Apparently he had been a customs agent in this community for 18 months and never processed a cruising boat! He would begin each call with a long conversation inquiring about the receiving person's family, children and respond with particulars about his life and family. These introductions lasted for five to 10 minutes before he would address the situation at hand. While we were all anxious to get the customs procedures over with, I found it heart-warming and refreshing to witness such engaging conversations where each person's family and their current well-being took precedence over their formal duties.

Both customs and immigration departments finally figured out their respective procedures and not only processed our entrance papers but also agreed to meet us on the pier the following day with our required departure papers. Our only cost was the price of the taxis between the offices. Clearly, I have never been treated so well by officials in any country. This was a pleasant and welcoming surprise.

This weather delay put our boats on new schedules. *Dragon's Toy* had an imminent departure date to transit the Panama Canal and *Sweetie* was content to take their time to explore all of the coastal communities throughout Central America. I was beginning to panic because my special friends, Noel and Jenny Villard, were meeting me in Panama with their flights booked to arrive on November 15 – only three weeks away. I was still struggling with a weakened immune system and numb limbs, so I could only manage to operate *Precious Metal* for a limited number of hours each day.

We agreed to abandon our harmonious foursome fleet and go our separate ways. Henry and I would continue day sailing as quickly as possible along the coast while *Sweetie* trailed behind at their own pace and *Dragon's Toy* raced for the Canal.

Henry and I settled into a comfortable pattern of weighing the anchor just before sunrise and covering approximately 50 miles each day. As the sun began to set each late afternoon we would head towards shore and set our anchors in approximately 50 feet of water. We gradually made our way along the entire Nicaraguan coast and into northern Costa Rica. Hand-steering for 12 hours each day became exhausting – particularly due to my compromised immune system. We stopped for one glorious full day in the isolated bay of Bahia Santa Elena on the northern tip of Costa Rica to wait for better weather. Here we enjoyed some wonderful snorkelling as well as fun celebrations with our friends, Dana and Kristen from Iceland (on the sailing vessel *Malita*) who announced to us that night that she was pregnant with their first child!

When we finally arrived into Cocos Harbour, in northern Costa Rica, I could no longer deal with my continued fatigue and reluctantly went to another doctor for more tests. Apparently, my white blood cell count was still extremely low and the doctor insisted that I needed to rest. With utmost regret I was forced to contact Noel and Jenny and postpone their trip to Panama. We were all truly disappointed. There was simply nothing more I could do to reach Panama in time. From this point forward Henry and I changed our strategy and slowly worked our way towards Panama.

Not having a schedule had a profound change with respect to my outlook towards cruising. If we liked a village or anchorage, we simply stayed until we were ready to leave. Our days revolved around swimming, snorkelling, kayaking and beach walking. We collected new and unique shells from each of the islands that we explored. Riley loved his daily beach runs and began racing around the beaches hunting and chasing hermit crabs and local snails. We read books, listened to music, watched the sunsets and explored each village. Time became incidental. My health began to improve. I finally felt refreshed and able to commit to writing again. This became the cruising lifestyle that I cherished.

I finally discovered and understood what cruising is all about.

It took me several years to truly appreciate the importance of the cliché 'stopping to smell the roses'. All too often I've witnessed fellow cruisers who have rushed from one place to the next on some kind of rigid schedule and never took the time to appreciate their current location. I too emulated these characteristics in my first years of cruising largely due to my previous lifestyle in Canada when I was indoctrinated into filling every moment of my day and life. It takes time to adjust to a less frantic pace.

Time became something that we joked about in our cruising lifestyle. We've commonly had intense arguments over what day it was. In one anchorage a cruiser called on the radio in a serious voice, "Could someone please tell me what day it is?" Another person replied, "It's Saturday, February 24." There was silence. Another voice came on, "Are you sure? I thought it was Sunday." Eventually, after long bantering back and forth everyone unanimously agreed on Sunday.

Henry needed a mechanic when we first arrived into Costa Rica and set up an appointment for 8.30am on the following Wednesday. I watched him dinghy to the main dock to pick up the mechanic at the specified time and return 20 minutes later alone in his dinghy. I called and asked about the situation and Henry replied, "I discovered that it's only 7.30. We've been in Costa Rica for three days and never realized that we went through a time change." I laughed. "Aha!" I said. "I was wondering why everyone in the restaurant yesterday was still eating breakfast while I had ordered a hamburger and beer!"

Our final passage to Panama City was a 70-mile stretch across the Gulf of Panama. The weather was benign as we weighed anchor, but as the day unfolded the winds and seas began to build. By mid-afternoon we were pounding into huge seas, strong winds and progressing at less than three knots. Half way across, it was clear that we wouldn't make landfall by sunset so we decided to alter course and head for the Las Perlas Islands – 35 miles away. Gale force winds continued to build creating huge steep waves that were only seconds apart. By late afternoon we were fighting every adverse weather condition imaginable: thunder, lightning, torrential rain, gale force winds, steep waves on the beam and *Precious Metal* was rocking from side to side at 35 degree angles.

As nightfall was setting in I radioed to Henry saying, "Things aren't going well on *Precious Metal*. I can't point the boat high enough to get to the closest island of San Juan. My engine keeps dying because I'm rolling so hard. I may have to fall off the wind and drift for the night."

My shoulders and neck were sore from hand-steering and having to hold onto the wheel with such intensity. Henry patiently said that he would alter course and come closer to *Precious Metal*. Eventually, we were able to manoeuvre our boats into the protected lee of San Juan Island by 8.00pm. The seas calmed down immediately and the winds dissipated. I relied on Henry to navigate his boat ahead of mine through the rocky outcrops into the anchorage in quiet water. After securely anchoring, all I could think of was my comfortable bed. I treated myself to a celebratory glass of single malt scotch and after a warm relaxing bath I fell into a wonderful deep sleep.

Riley and I woke up in absolute paradise. We were surrounded by brilliant blue skies, strikingly beautiful lush green vegetation with numerous white sandy beaches, deep turquoise water and enormous rock formations scattered throughout the entrance that we navigated through the previous evening in total darkness. I was overwhelmed by the realization that I was anchored in a bay that boasted such magnificent beauty.

The extreme contrast between the previous night's storm and the tranquillity of my surroundings was astounding. What was I thinking? Ironically, 12 hours earlier I had been wondering why I had ever considered subjecting myself to such an uncomfortable and challenging situation. I subsequently woke up in paradise and asked myself how I had ever considered abandoning the opportunity of experiencing such a miraculous and meaningful lifestyle.

Inside Precious Metal *after the storm*

CHAPTER 14

Pamela in Panama: Finally!

December 2011

SEEING IS BELIEVING. No amount of photographs or reading prepared me for the sight ahead of me as *Precious Metal* approached the outskirts of Panama City. An incredible number of massive freighters and ships were milling in the distance waiting for their turn to enter the Panama Canal. My radar was completely filled with dots marking the ships and I was suddenly on high alert wondering how I would possibly navigate through the pack. Five miles before my destination, a huge storm descended on the region which made it difficult to see further then my bow. The winds were howling along with torrential rains making the situation even more tenuous.

Precious Metal seemed so insignificant in comparison to the humongous ships around me. Knowing they all had the right of way made the navigation even more intense. Even more challenging was that some ships were at anchor, some were coming towards me and some were heading away. Using my binoculars I intently tried to assess each ship and its course of action through the blinding rain and fog. Furthermore, I had never been into the popular cruisers' anchorage called Las Brisas where at least 50 sailboats were swinging wildly on their anchors. Henry and I took turns leading each other through the fleet and finally found a secure place to set our anchors.

Storms are intense but short-lived in Panama and soon the skies opened allowing me to sit back in my cockpit with a much needed glass of chilled white wine and absorb the scenery. The city skyline was impressive with massive highrises that have been designed by numerous famous architects. Despite the recent world recession, Panama has been experiencing a booming economy due to the continuing traffic through the canal for nearly 100 years (the 100th anniversary is in 2014 when they will celebrate the opening of a second canal adjacent to the current one).

Panama is a somewhat cosmopolitan country largely attributed to the wide variety of immigrants who have settled there. It has a fascinating history; particularly relating to the treacherous development of the canal and the nations that have controlled the construction project over the past 100 years. Panama has recently opened its doors to retiring ex-pats who have discovered an inexpensive lifestyle in a comfortable climate with a multitude of amenities and activities. There's something for everyone in Panama.

Sadly, this bustling economy seems to have grown at an unmanageable pace which presents notable shortcomings. Traffic was unbearable during peak hours due to continual construction of the necessary infrastructure to support the expansion. Garbage, improper sanitation services and lack of proper fuel emission requirements in vehicles were all environmentally disturbing. Police seemed unwilling or unable to cope with the level of crime that's associated with drugs, money laundering and (I suspect) the multitude of many other undesirable types of behaviour which I couldn't even think about. While my personal safety was never challenged, I felt I always that I needed to be on guard and looking over my shoulder.

That said, I will always cherish my 10 months in Panama. Henry and I fell into a routine whereby we would spend two to three weeks exploring the Las Perlas Islands, 35 miles south of the city, followed by several days in the city to re-provision and make whatever repairs we needed to our boats. The islands boast minimal development, making our lifestyle a comfortable blend of solitude and city life. We often joked that together we owned a trimaran: *Rapscullion* was our social, dining and sleeping quarters; whereas *Precious Metal* was considered to be the office (where I did my writing), fitness centre and spa – in light of my decadent bathtub.

Riley far preferred Henry's catamaran because it was more stable and provided more places to lounge. Plus, Riley always received many more treats from Henry than from me. Henry also spoiled Riley with kayak excursions each day to the beach. Riley would sit proudly like royalty on our kayak that was tied to Henry's waist as we snorkelled around the coral reefs and and he would swim to the beach for his daily run and crab hunt.

Almost immediately after my arrival in Panama I began contacting Garmin Industries in the United States to sort out my autopilot situation. A nice man in the service department named Caleb became sympathetic to my situation and was eventually instrumental in solving the devastating occurrence. We first agreed that I should ship my new unit back to the factory and they replaced it. Months went by before I received the replacement forcing me to continue hand-steering back and forth to the islands. (This delay was not Garmin's fault. The original unit was hand delivered to Garmin by my friend Bruce who came to visit and I picked it up several months later when I flew to North America.)

Much to my dismay and displeasure my replacement autopilot did not work. The one-year anniversary of hand-steering came and went and I consequently lost my patience. What was I thinking? I needed to put my foot down and stop being so nice.

Poor Caleb witnessed a side of me that few people are ever exposed to when I finally became angry and wrote my 'action letter'. By this time, through extensive research, I discovered that Gabriel at Marinsa in El Salvador knowingly ordered an autopilot pump that was incompatible for my boat. I had obtained the emails between Garmin and Gabriel where Garmin stated in writing, "This pump is not suitable for a 50,000-pound sailboat; rather, it's made for a small powerboat." Despite

Garmin's recommendations, Gabriel ordered the pump the following day – which is why my new autopilot didn't function. I also discovered that Garmin didn't make a suitable pump for my boat. I was livid. The fatigue and discomfort that Gabriel caused was beyond belief.

My action letter was written and emailed to every Garmin executive in the world who had influence, including the CEO, legal advisor, chairman of sales and marketing, as well as the chairman of service. I explained the entire situation and attached the written emails between Garmin and Marinsa as evidence for fraud and/or gross misrepresentation. I also mentioned that I'm a writer and listed the publications that I would be sending submissions to (including a list of their respective circulation numbers which amounted to a readership of over 100,000) if they didn't have a new, functioning autopilot on my boat immediately. Within one week, a new custom-made pump was constructed and delivered to Panama and the entire unit was functioning magically! At last, I was free to enjoy sailing without having to hand-steer.

My friends Howard and Lynn from Vancouver (on their boat *Swift Current*) were travelling with us in Panama at the time and supported of my actions with Garmin. Howard is a retired lawyer and when the new functioning autopilot was installed he remarked, "Pamela, you should send a copy of your action letter to Harvard Business School!"

My 15-year-old dinghy was getting tired and needed to be pumped up every morning and night, so I finally decided that it was time to find a replacement. The 'Dinghy Doctor' in Panama City came to my rescue with what appeared to be a suitable second-hand dinghy. After I inspected their dinghy in their shop, I agreed to pay $1,200.00 as long as they deliver it to the anchorage. What was I thinking? It took the better part of the afternoon to switch the motor mount and wheel mounts from my old dinghy to the new one. Tears ran down my cheeks as I bid farewell to my old dinghy that had served me so wonderfully well throughout my travels.

I thanked the young man for looking after me so well and headed out to *Precious Metal* in my new dinghy. Less than five minutes passed and the entire floor deflated. The seam around the air intake valve blew open and I had no floor support. I managed to get to my boat and immediately called the store to report that my dinghy had a huge leak. "I will have to speak with my partner," said the young man. "I will call you tomorrow."

Several emails and unanswered phone calls later, I finally reached my 'Dinghy Doctor' representative who advised me that, "My partner thinks you may have put the hole in the dinghy." "What? Why would I do that?" I exclaimed. "I think you need a new partner!" He told me not to take it personally and that he would refund $850.00, but he was not going to exchange the dinghies again at the nearby boat ramp. I would have to come to a boat ramp closer to his store which was part way up the entrance to the Panama Canal and I had two days to remove my old dinghy from his store or no money would be refunded.

We created quite a scene the following day because boats aren't allowed past a certain area in the canal unless they are transiting and the destined boat ramp was a long way into the restricted area. I was intent on getting my money back and certainly didn't want the malfunctioning dinghy. As we towed Henry's dinghy and the derelict dinghy under the famous Bridge of Americas (which unites North and South America) numerous canal working boats and police boats approached us screaming at us to turn around. I pretended not to understand Spanish, English or any of the languages they yelled in and continued to navigate forward. Panamanian sport boats are allowed to dry dock using the boat ramp but they have to have an accredited pass to do so.

We finally arrived at the designated boat ramp about a mile up the canal passage and Henry quickly used his dinghy to go ashore, change the motor and wheel mounts back onto my old dinghy while I hovered in very shallow water at the side of the canal driving *Precious Metal* in tiny circles. Huge freighters and container ships passed by within 20 feet of my boat. The canal working boats continued to approach me and scream. I held little Riley in my arms and pleaded innocence, repeating, "*No comprendo!*" It seemed to take forever for Henry to return, towing my dinghy behind his, but we had success. Once both dinghies were attached, I turned *Precious Metal* and gunned the throttle in full force towards the Bridge of Americas.

This $350.00 exercise was a lesson learned. What was I thinking? I should have insisted on testing the second-hand dinghy before payment. I subsequently ordered a brand new model from Florida and was in possession the following week. She's named *Precious Gem* and she proudly rides like a sports car. Dinghies play an important role on a cruising boat because they act as our cars to take us to shore and everywhere we need to venture. Fortunately, I saved over $1,000.00 by purchasing it in Panama versus another country, so in essence I was able to recover my loss.

During my stay in Panama I observed that most of the cruising boats rarely linger; they are usually there to transit the canal except for a handful of boats that have made it their (quasi) permanent home. Henry and I had long debates whether to transit the canal and head to Columbia and the western Caribbean or return to Mexico. I longed to return to Mexico and the cruiser-friendly lifestyle that it provides. "If I go through the canal, I will feel as though I'm going the wrong way," I repeated time and time again. Not only did I miss Mexico and its amenities, but it would be closer and easier to travel to visit my friends and family in Canada.

I was clearly becoming homesick for familiar friends and family and tired of the challenges of Third World countries. During my five-year voyage I had returned to Canada at least twice a year to visit family and friends and visited my son Sam (including my wonderful daughter-in-law Lizz and two adorable young grandchildren Maddy and George) at their home in London, England, each year. My son Charlie and his lovely wife Catherine also visited me from Newfoundland for Christmas in Panama. Numerous friends devoted their holidays towards visiting aboard *Precious Metal* over the five-year span. I was also fortunate to live in an era when communication devices allowed daily contact with my loved ones (when I was in places that had Internet).

Mexico always represented a wonderful blend of comfortable amenities, interesting culture, cruiser-friendly anchorages and a meaningful cruising community of sailors who don't venture too far away from their homes in North America. I had no regrets about my experiences in the distant waters of Central America, South America and Panama; but it was time to go home – or at least closer to home. To my delight, in late September Henry and I finally decided to buddy boat together back to Mexico. We anxiously prepared our boats for departure the following week.

I had one last item on my 'wish-list' before departing Panama – to transit the Panama Canal. My timing could not have been better, because Howard and Lynn were scheduled to take *Swift Current* through the canal the following week and asked me to be one of their line-handlers. This was a true honour for me. We experienced the Panama Canal at its very best with terrific weather, charming pilots and a wonderful crew of friends. Line-handling was an exciting task and somewhat demanding. We made it through the canal in one glorious day and had a driver waiting to take me back to Panama City.

My emotions were running high with glee as I prepared *Precious Metal* for her final 1,400-mile voyage back to southern Mexico. Many long days and nights were devoted towards checking and re-checking every system aboard the boat until I was convinced that she was completely ship-shape. Like a horse running back to the barn, I made my final stop to re-fuel and left Panama City in the background as I headed out to sea. We planned to spend one more evening anchored in the Las Perlas Islands which would reduce our mileage across the Gulf of Panama. Ironically, the very last freighter that I passed as I wound my way through the fleet was named the M/V *Pamela*!

Heading Back to Mexico: The Grand Finale!

Precious Metal behaved perfectly across the 35-mile stretch to the Las Perlas Islands that day. Not having to hand-steer was a wonderful bonus. My euphoria was short-lived once I arrived at our anchorage and I heard the sound of water gushing into my engine room through the drive shaft. I quickly noticed that the hose clamps on the base of the drive shaft had rusted apart and needed to be replaced. "Boats will always keep us humble," I said to myself as I located the proper-sized hose clamps from my spare part cabinet and prepared myself for a challenging job. My arms weren't long enough to reach the drive shaft so I was forced to dismantle the heat exchanger in order to barely reach. I was upside-down and in a contortionist position for nearly an hour until I finally and successfully secured the new clamps.

What I didn't realize was that I accidentally and inadvertently nudged the fuel return valve slightly closed as I was grovelling upside-down with the hose clamps. In my haste to prepare dinner and congratulate myself on the success with the hose clamps I never thought to check all valves in the surrounding area that I was working. What was I thinking?

We departed our anchorage at sunrise the following morning along with a fabulous farewell show by local porpoises. I was in my glory heading out to sea watching a magnificent sunrise as I sipped my morning coffee.

Approximately 30 miles into the voyage I was doing my usual rounds of gauges and noticed that my fuel was low. This didn't make sense because my tanks were full when I left Panama City a day earlier. I radioed to Henry and explained my concern and we both agreed that the gauge was likely failing. After all, my water gauges often indicated incorrect measurements. "According to this gauge I have two hours of fuel left," I said. Meanwhile we were travelling through the busiest area of freighter traffic heading towards and away from the Canal.

My engine died exactly two hours after that call. I was baffled. Where did the fuel go? It clearly wasn't coming out of the bilge and leaving a trail behind the boat. The seas were relatively calm so I lowered my dinghy and went to Henry's boat to borrow 13 gallons of fuel from him, plus I had 10 extra jerry cans of diesel aboard *Precious Metal*. Still mystified, we continued onwards. I usually allow for five miles to the gallon and was consuming one mile to the gallon. In desperation I cut the hose from the filter system and put it directly into the jerry cans thinking that I possibly had a blockage in the fuel line. By 7.30pm that evening my engine once again died and all of the extra jerry cans were empty.

Fortunately, the wind rose just in time to allow a nice beam reach across the remaining 30 miles to the opposite shore of the Gulf of Panama. At 1.30am I anchored *Precious Metal* under sail at an open roadstead in 50 feet of water with *Rapscullion* anchored 50 feet away. I barely slept that night wondering and wondering: what could possibly be wrong? Where on earth was my fuel going?

We woke up early and to my surprise and delight I had cell phone coverage. I telephoned my mechanic Ernie at Klassen Motors in Canada as soon as his store was opened. He immediately advised me that the fuel return line also needed to be cut and placed into the jerry can. What was I thinking? It immediately dawned on me that I must have kicked the return valve to my main fuel tank closed when I was struggling to put the hose clamps on the drive shaft. Sure enough, the fuel return valve was marginally off centre and all of the diesel had been going into my keel tank that had been closed off for years! (Engines use the fuel it needs and returns the surplus back into the tank that it is drawing from.) In this case, because the valve was closed to my main tank, the fuel went into my alternate tank.

After much discussion, Henry and I regretfully decided that the prudent strategy would be to return to Panama City. My fuel filter lines needed to be cleaned out due to the sludge from the bottom of the tank that likely got into the lines when I ran out of fuel. I could not use the fuel that was in my secondary tank because it would definitely be dirty after many years of sitting idle. Before attempting the long voyage back to Panama City I needed to obtain more fuel. During the previous night I noticed lights from a tiny village 10 miles in the distance so we raised our anchors and sailed in that direction.

The small fishing village of Puerto Mensabe is located on a large estuary that shallows at least a mile into the ocean. We anchored both boats a long way from shore and took our dinghy into their fairly substantial pier with all of the empty jerry cans that both boats owned. We were greeted with enthusiasm and one fellow offered to drive our jugs 20 miles to the next town to obtain the 30 gallons of fuel. While we were waiting for his return, five officials approached us on the pier and suspiciously began asking us questions. They all wore very stern looks and took their questioning seriously.

We were then ushered in a van to the navy office and asked for our papers and passports which had been left on our boats – since we were only coming to shore for fuel. Eventually they called in the navy ship and by this time at least 20 uniformed officials were milling around the building. Twelve officials with their M16 rifles boarded the navy ship with us and took us to our boats for inspection and paperwork. We were suddenly being treated as criminals. This gruelling process lasted for five and a half hours as each official filled out their respective forms, took photographs of the boats and the forms and tried to find something amiss.

I continued to worry about my fuel that was supposed to be delivered to the pier. I was permitted to collect the fuel and then told to return to their office for further processing of forms. They finally released us at 7.30pm to navigate our way back to our boats in a hazardous channel in the dark. I politely asked the captain of the navy ship to safely lead us out of the channel but he was given orders not to. We finally arrived back at our boats totally disillusioned by our experience. I still had to load the jerry cans into my engine room compartment. My back was sore, I was exhausted and my 'Eau de Diesel' fragrance from being immersed in fuel for the past 24 hours permeated the entire boat! Thank heavens for my bathtub.

Having to return to Panama City was disheartening for both of us. I called my friend John on the boat *Millennium* who was waiting for our arrival and who agreed to help me clean the fuel lines. Once again, only several days after our original departure, we re-fuelled and set out to sea feeling a sense of déjà vu. "What more could go wrong?" I asked myself. What was I thinking?

Our first few days after departing Panama City for the second time went smoothly. We rounded the dreaded Punto Mala (which means 'Bad Point') reasonably well. Punta Mala is a confluence of several weather systems and currents that make the ride uncomfortable for several hours. After Punto Mala, there is another 60 miles of choppy, uncomfortable seas and rugged coastline to the first available anchorage. We anchored comfortably in the first protected, designated anchorage in a rainy, overcast bay hoping for a relaxing night. That was not to be.

The worst storm that I have ever experienced at anchor arose early that evening. It was an intense local storm and not mentioned on any of my weather resources. *Precious Metal* was being tossed and turned from every angle. The swells were so high that I often could not see Henry's boat 50 feet away due to the massive troughs of the swells. Green water was crashing over the bow and sometimes landed in the cockpit. My anchor snubber (a resilient line that absorbs the anchor tension) snapped so that with each swell the sound of the anchor being yanked against the steel hull resonated throughout the boat.

My mind was fearful that these occasions are when a weak anchor chain link is fully tested and could snap, sending *Precious Metal* crashing into the surrounding reefs. My dinghy lines (in the davits) had so much torque that several security lines broke causing the new dinghy to swing wildly behind *Precious Metal*. There was nothing I could do – it was too dangerous to go on deck. I stayed on watch until the system weakened at 1.00am and finally poured myself a much-needed scotch.

We set out the next morning at dawn, bound for Santa Catalina which is 35 miles away. After lifting the anchor and heading away from the bay I suddenly noticed that I had no steerage. By this time we were in 100 feet of water outside the anchorage. Once I was clear of a lee shore, I checked my rudder compartment and discovered that the three-quarter-inch thick bronze arm that attaches the rudder to the steering arm was cracked completely in half. The boat's violent crashing about during the previous night's storm caused incredible pressure on this integral part of the steering system. I alerted Henry by radio and then tied off the steering arm to allow me to steer in one direction – to port. Then I performed huge circles to port until I was in finally in water shallow enough to anchor.

By this time, the swell size had increased and was too tumultuous to launch a dinghy, so Henry had to come to my boat on his kayak. Using my grinder, wood blocks and hose clamps we jury-rigged a concoction that braced the bronze arm together – albeit knowingly tenuously, given the huge size of my rudder and the forces against it in large seas.

There are only three times in my life when I have literally been scared at sea: once in Japan in the late 1980s, once single-handing with surfing waves into a challenging anchorage at dusk in Alaska and most notably on this day. I considered using my jury-rigged emergency tiller which secures to the rudder shaft but this required steering from below (under my bunk) and therefore I would not be able to see outside. This emergency rudder would not suitable for a single-hander except in a dire emergency.

The following seven hours tested every bit of my internal strength. I was totally on edge as I pounded 35 miles through fairly steep waves on the beam solely dependent on our jury-rigged concoction. Making matters worse was the lee shore that was lined with rocky outcrops. Naturally, I gave it a wide berth and Henry was continuously calling by radio with support. We both knew that if those tiny hose clamps gave way I was in very deep trouble. At times I was nauseous from fear and other times I simply found myself shaking. It took everything I had to stay calm and composed.

Two famous lifetime quotes from my youth as a national-level gymnast came to the forefront during this episode: "When the going gets tough, the tough get going," and, "Champions were all once contenders who just never gave up." I suspect I repeated these quotes at least 50 times that day to keep my sanity intact and my mind focused.

I finally anchored safely in the protected bay of Santa Catalina. There was nothing more comforting than feeling the anchor tug securely into the ocean floor after my harrowing day at sea. The following morning I dismantled the broken rudder quadrant and headed into town to find a welder. Local residents were encouraging and said in Spanish that a competent welder was just down the road, about 20 minutes by car. "How fortunate is this?" I thought. Never expecting the solution to my broken rudder quadrant would be so easy. What was I thinking?

After realizing that no cars were passing I hailed the local school bus and the driver happily invited me on board. About 30 young uniformed school children stared at me in silence the entire way wondering what this gringo lady was doing on their bus? The kind driver dropped me off right in front of the welder's house and soon disappeared. I suddenly realized that I was in the middle of nowhere. Furthermore, the welder took one look at the quadrant and shook his head. My interpretation of his Spanish was that he didn't have the materials to weld bronze and I would have to go to Santiago which was 120 miles away.

I stood on the side of the road waiting for any vehicle to pass by and after 30 minutes I was hungry and disillusioned. Many horses passed me, making me wonder if I would have to take a horse? I stopped one cowboy-looking man riding a healthy-looking stallion and asked how long it would take to go to Santiago? He looked at me with an outrageous glare and shook his head as he trotted away. Finally, a decrepit-looking car arrived and stopped close by. I quickly approached it and asked the driver in Spanish, "Are you a taxi?" He paused for a second, thought about it and finally said, "Yes!" "How much will it cost to go to Santiago?" I asked. "Sixty dollars." I agreed to his price and proceeded to climb into his broken-down quasi-vehicle when he turned and said, "*Manana.*" (Tomorrow) Frantically, I reached into my wallet and handed him $75.00. He looked at the money, paused, turned on the ignition and we were off to Santiago.

My life came before me a number of times on this journey. The floor below my feet had rotted and I could see the road below as we zoomed around the corners at high speeds. My driver, Rudolfo, was highly entertaining and full of life as we both managed to converse in each other's languages. Fortunately, he knew of a competent welder in Santiago who was able to do the repair overnight. For another $75.00 Rudolfo agreed to take me back to the boat that night and bring the rudder quadrant to Santa Catalina the following day.

Rudolfo went far beyond his call of during as a driver and by 2.00pm the following day my welded part was in my hands. Ironically, the fellow did a masterful job at welding but broke the ball off the top of the part that secures the arm for the autopilot. I immediately panicked dreading that I would once again have to hand-steer. Thankfully, with more hose clamps and ingenuity, Henry and I created another concoction that allowed the autopilot to work, at least temporarily.

Western Panama boasts some spectacular island groups scattered approximately 20 miles apart with lovely white sand beaches and great exploring. We spent one night each in two of these island groups before heading into Boca Chica – which is on the mainland of western Panama. Panama's second largest city of David is only an hour drive from Boca Chica and we needed to re-provision.

The narrow 8-mile channel into Boca Chica is not marked and requires tremendous vigilance to avoid many reefs, shallow waters and strong currents. We were well prepared with three guide books, our chart plotters and computerized charts marking our various fixes along the route. Checking and re-checking, Henry usually goes ahead of me in difficult situations because he only draws (keel depth) four feet and I draw seven. Therefore, if he came across an area that was too shallow for me I would have time to turn around. Most of Panama is poorly charted or not at all – except for the region around the canal.

We did a masterful job of navigating the entire channel on a rising tide – which is prudent. Suddenly, just in front of the tiny town we got caught in a strong current. Within seconds I noticed Henry's mast had knocked and severed an unmarked power line. I quickly looked up to see if there were other power lines above and then Henry called on the radio saying he had hit ground. It all happened so fast.

I tried to steer around him in the raging current and ran straight up onto an unmarked reef. The current was so strong that it continued to bounce *Precious Metal* sideways along the reef – what a horrible feeling and sound! Finally she stopped, sitting sideways on the reef heeling at 35 degrees with the forces of the current rushing around the boat. At 35 degrees *Precious Metal's* hull buried the port holes (which were locked) and furnace exhaust (which was plugged) and there was about one inch of hull visible below the deck line.

I took a few seconds to collect my thoughts. At this point Henry was able to release his boat into safety of the nearby channel. Some local residents came to my rescue in their power boat and said they would try to find assistance. My bilges were clear of water and the hull was intact. It would be three hours before high slack tide, when, with any good fortune, *Precious Metal* would float again. Thankfully, *Precious Metal's* 'precious metal' once again saved me.

I continued to call on Channel 16 for assistance and a wonderful man named Carlos came to my rescue as well as another cruising boat (Bill, who I had worked with several years prior at Sail Fest in Zihuatanejo aboard *Some Day*) in his dinghy. Soon, Henry was able to anchor and also be on hand. Carlos set my anchor in the channel. We tried many strategies to tug *Precious Metal* off the reef but we needed the tide to rise and more water below the boat.

Gradually the boat righted from 35 degrees to 30 to 25 to 20. At first the engine was working but eventually it would not turn over. I bled the fuel system which was enough to get the engine running once she was level and free of the reef.

Suddenly, at exactly 2.00pm when the tide reached its height and the current was slack, *Precious Metal* swung on her anchor and released from the reef. It took some very quick manoeuvring to bring up the anchor and head into safety with Carlos leading the way. He took me to a small anchorage in front of his house. I could not backtrack up the channel to where Henry was anchored because one power line was still intact and at high tide I would have wiped it out. Carlos dove under the boat and checked for any damage. A few scrapes in the paint was all he could find. I treated my rescuers to dinner at a lovely restaurant that evening and unwound with some tasty margaritas!

People say that things happen in threes, although I wasn't mentally prepared for three major challenges in my first 10 days of departing Panama! I learned to no longer ask myself, "What more can go wrong?" After a few fun-filled days in Boca Chica

Precious Metal *high and dry on the sand bar in Boca Chica*

we decided to spend a week in recouping in the idyllic Western Panama islands before heading back to one of my favourite anchorages in Golfito, Costa Rica, where we re-united with many friends from that region.

After departing Golfito, *Rapscullion* and *Precious Metal* both enjoyed fabulous sailing each day as we ventured north along the spectacular and lush Costa Rica coastline. I was in heaven with glorious winds and both sails flying. Everything was almost perfect until the day we approached Cocos Harbour on the northern tip of the country. I was preparing lunch in the galley and routinely surfaced to check the horizon. To my surprise, I was heading out to sea! I quickly checked my autopilot and saw that the rudder indicator was no longer centred. A sinking feeling came over me. I raced to the rudder compartment under my bed and found that the recently welded quadrant was once again cracked – right beside the newly welded area. Not again!

I stopped the engine and called to Henry with my disappointing news. At least I knew what to do this time. Without hesitation I tied the steering arm to a support under the bed and steered in giant circles to port towards land. Once again, Henry came to my rescue and after our anchors were in 40 feet, he kayaked to my boat. Practice makes perfect and in no time we had jury-rigged another concoction of wood splints and hose clamps to secure the quadrant onto the rudder shaft. We felt like pros! We had 20 miles to Cocos Harbour and the delay pressed us for time if we wanted to arrive by nightfall.

The winds and seas began to build as we navigated down the final channel towards Cocos Harbour. Soon we were pounding into the waves and I never thought we'd get there. Darkness set in making navigation difficult amongst the fishing pangas that were heading out to sea for the night. Just as we approached the entrance to the Harbour, I lost my steering entirely. Suddenly, I was entering a busy harbour at night in a storm with no steering. I was tired, anxious and praying that I could control *Precious Metal* until I was in a reasonable depth to drop my anchor.

The hose clamps were still tight but the quadrant had cracked a third time. Metal fatigue had obviously set in and I would need a brand new quadrant to be fabricated. Henry led me through the pack of *pangas*, ploughing the way so they would move aside as I came through. Fortunately the wind was behind us so I could go straight but could not turn. When I reached a 50 foot depth I immediately dropped my anchor knowing that *Precious Metal* would be in that location until a new rudder quadrant was made.

There's no better place to be stuck for a week then Cocos Harbour. Thankfully, a wonderful company named Three Gringos recently settled there from the United States and had established an impressive machine shop only two blocks from the beach. During the time that they masterfully fabricated a new quadrant we became terrific friends with the family (Dennis, Janine and Dennis Jr) and re-acquainted ourselves with some wonderful cruising friends in the anchorage. We had a scrumptious Thanksgiving feast aboard our friend's fabulous power boat *Elysium* (Deb and Jewell) and several other meaningful friends.

The following three weeks were, in fact, problem-free. *Precious Metal* was on her best behaviour through Nicaragua, Guatemala and finally into Marina Chiapas, Puerto Madera, Mexico. Henry and I tooted each of our horns in delight as we crossed the Guatemala–Mexico border on December 17 marking a momentous occasion. We were finally back home in Mexico.

I will be the first to admit that Henry and I had some major challenges in our relationship during the course of our 20 months of buddy boating. After all, we're both single-handers with very strong minds. What were we thinking? We were terrific together in terms of boating and the appreciation for our cruising lifestyle. Our boats travelled at similar speeds and we always agreed on navigation, safety issues and choices of locations to stop as well as our duration of stay in each place.

He was always incredibly genuine, caring, romantic and attentive and cooked me dinner every single night. We've shared highs and lows in our two years together that few couples would ever experience. Typical of most cruisers, he has always been reluctant to make any kind of a commitment; so the future of our relationship has always been a mystery, but by the end of our voyage to Mexico we were having a lot of fun together.

Our timing into Puerto Madero was uncanny. During the two years that I had been exploring Central America, the hype surrounding the end of the Mayan Calendar on December

(Left to right): Henry, Pamela and our great friend Paul from S/V Sun Runner *enjoying a wonderful feast with our Canadian friends, Jeanne Harvey and Brian Johnston, at their lovely home in La Manzanilla, Mexico.*

21, 2012, was a dominant theme. I encountered a number of people who were convinced that the world was coming to an end on December 21. Palenque, one of the most famous Mayan archaeological sites and a World Heritage Site dating back to between the 3rd and 5th century, is near Puerto Madero – which is where we spent our first week in Mexico waiting for a storm to pass in the Gulf of Tehuantepec.

Henry and I made a special effort to visit the ancient ruins of Palenque on December 21 to embrace the Mayan celebration that ended one of the cycles of the Mayan calendar. The ceremonies and subdued atmosphere was somewhat spiritual and tastefully coordinated. If you're reading this book it's clear that the world did not come to an end as many people proposed.

"Isn't this fitting?" I said to Henry as we walked through the various paths around the archaeological ruins. "Now that we're back in Mexico, I feel that this chapter of my sailing adventures has been fulfilled. I've experienced so much and learned an

We were privileged to attend the sacred Mayan celebration marking the end of their historic calendar on December 21, 2012.

enormous amount about cruising, life, myself and the wonderful world that we live in. With respect to the Mayan culture that has surrounded and embraced me for so many years, this may not be the end of the world, but it's a perfect place to end my book. Just like in the Mayan calendar, I don't believe that it's the end; rather, a brand new beginning."

As we walked down the long road to the highway in silence I contemplated where in the world this new beginning would lead me?

EPILOGUE

Log Entry: Zihutanejo, Mexico

March 1, 2013

PRECIOUS METAL – I guess you should be the first to find this out. I never imagined that I'd be writing this, but I've decided to take you back to Canada and retire you from cruising life. Tears stream down my cheeks as I enter this log, because we both always thought we'd be cruising the world together until my final days. Please understand that I'm doing this for you. Let's face it – you're a woman: high maintenance and expensive!

The places we've explored, the people we've met and the experiences we've shared are so monumental: circumnavigating Vancouver Island, exploring the coast of Alaska, Mexico many times, Galapagos, Peru, Cocos Islands, Central America and also Panama – something like 25,000 ocean miles. You've given me my lifetime dream. Together we made it happen and I'm so incredibly grateful. You have never let me down.

This is likely a hiccup in my cruising life and I'll be back on the sea in no time. There are so many aspects to this lifestyle that suit me. I love the fact that I virtually leave no footprint on the planet. I love my cruising friends – despite the horrible inevitability of always having to say good-bye. I love waking up and putting my bikini on – never wearing shoes, a sweater, or long pants. I love being unencumbered; you don't need many things when you live aboard a boat – except tools! I love being at one with Mother Nature. I love knowing that I can travel to anywhere in the world that's beside an ocean. This lifestyle provides a peaceful sense of awareness that is almost impossible to capture in an urban environment.

This journey has also taught me so many lessons about life beyond sailing:

- I've learned to never give up and that there will always be wonderful rewards for perseverance.
- I've learned that family, friends and purpose are most important in my life.
- I've learned how to stop and smell the roses.
- I've learned to be content with my own presence.
- I've learned that when one door closes another one opens.
- I've learned to always wear a hat and sunblock.
- I've learned to respect all sectors of humanity regardless of race, religion, or economic status.
- I've learned that doctors, dentists and professionals are conscientious everywhere world.
- I've learned that rust and mould never sleep, along with miraculous techniques to remove both.
- I've learned not to believe everything I read or hear.
- I've learned that every major challenge in life has a silver lining.
- I've learned how to change my oil without spilling a drop and how to change a fuel filter in less than a minute.
- I've learned patience and humility.
- I've learned that fear can cripple peoples' outlook and choices in life.
- I've learned that knowledge is power and alleviates most fear.
- I've learned that it's OKAY when my fingernails aren't manicured.
- I've learned to respect by body and stay fit in order to be physically able to accomplish my dreams.
- I've learned to walk with one eye watching the pavement in developing countries so I don't fall into nasty

potholes or off unsafe curbs.

- I've learned respect for our oceans and planet and how to live within sound, sustainable standards.
- I've learned that we don't have to wash our dishes in hot water; just rinse well. (I've been washing in cold water for years.)
- I've learned that this life is not a rehearsal and it's very short.
- I've learned that we don't need to put mayonnaise in the fridge.
- I've learned that western society devotes too much time to their hand-held gadgets.
- I've learned that most people in life are dreamers and that very few are goers.
- I learned that being a Grandma is the very best feeling.
- I've learned that money does not buy happiness.
- I've learned that I can drink crappy wine as long as it's cold.
- I've learned Not to get my hair done in low-end salons.
- I've learned that tequila is a good remedy for most illnesses!
- I've learned that it's wonderful to be a Canadian.
- I've learned Not to judge a restaurant by its appearance. Some trendy up-scale restaurants have mediocre food, whereas local basic eateries can be exceptionally good.
- I've learned that 99.9 percent of the people on this planet are wonderful, all trying to get through life the best way they know how with what they've been given.
- I've learned that we can't tame the sea, but we can challenge the waves of change in our lives.
- I've learned that the world is full of challenging opportunities, wonderful places and interesting people.
- I've learned that integrity and respect are the two most important ingredients for a harmonious global society.

Now my dream is to work towards promoting greater awareness in the world with regards to our ocean crisis, publish my book and pursue my love for writing. A wonderful sense of peacefulness lies within me as I ponder my decision to return to Canada. You'll make a terrific home for Riley and me as we return to traditional society. You've helped me realize that we can live our dreams and accomplish anything we want in life. I'm just so grateful that together, we had the wherewithal to make it happen and we never gave up.

APPENDIX I

Japan: An Untold Story

July 1989

I S IT TOO late to share one of my most memorable sailing tales that took place nearly a quarter century ago? While this saga took place when I was a young wife and mother of two young boys (ages 7 and 13), many aspects of this episode continue to re-surface in my mind, particularly as I write this current manuscript. The story of our family's eight-month voyage throughout Japan could be the foundation of an entire book, but for the purposes of this Appendix, I will simply describe the most interesting highlights of my two months alone as a single, blonde, female aboard my sailing vessel *Kluane* in Japan.

After over two years of sailing around the South Pacific aboard *Kluane* with my former husband Michael and two young sons Sam and Charlie, we finally re-united with my parents over dinner in their luxurious West Vancouver home. We had barely exchanged our initial pleasantries when the telephone rang. The caller was *Kluane*'s hired skipper who was supposed to be sailing her across the North Pacific Ocean to meet us in Alaska. Instead, he was phoning from Hokkaido Island in northern Japan and announced that the head stay (the wire cable that supports the mast from the bow) had broken 80 miles out of Osaka, forcing him to return to Japan. Furthermore, he advised me that he would be doubling his fees if we wanted him to continue our quest to have *Kluane* repaired and delivered to Alaska.

After much debate our only recourse was for me to return to Japan alone to sort out *Kluane's* problems. Both boys were scheduled to begin school in September and Michael had accepted an OB/GYN position in Chilliwack, British Columbia, beginning late August. Therefore *Kluane's* ultimate fate was in my hands. Less than two days after the phone call from our skipper, I had re-packed my belongings, purchased return flights to North America for the skipper and two crew, secured ample travellers cheques for an extended stay in Japan (which was the best option for financing travel in those days), said farewell to my husband, children and close family and friends for an undetermined amount of time. Before I knew it, I was sitting on a flight bound for Tokyo, Japan.

Our skipper advised me that he would take *Kluane* from Hokkaido to a small bay in the town of Misaki – 60 miles south of Yokohama (which is another one hour drive from Tokyo). I contacted Japan's representative of Seven Seas Sailing Association in advance of my flight and he dutifully agreed to escort me from Narita Airport to my boat, despite the fact that he was separating from his wife the following morning. Now that's a dedicated representative! I would probably still be looking for *Kluane* to this day without his kind offer, because signage and directions are impossible to interpret in Japan without an understanding of the language.

Immediately upon my arrival aboard *Kluane*, I handed our crew their airline tickets and they were off the boat within 30 minutes. I was left with no food, empty diesel and gas tanks, a broken head stay, a torn head sail and a boat that was disgustingly filthy. This was to be the first of many occasions in Japan that I simply sat down and cried.

After gathering myself together, my first task the following morning was to take *Kluane* into the fuel dock for diesel and gasoline. I still remember bringing the boat into the fuel dock and having no assistance with my lines from onlookers in the marina – they simply stared in amazement as though they weren't sure what to do with this blonde, single female who appeared with her sailboat out of nowhere. I managed to handle all of the manoeuvres on my own to dock the boat only to discover they wouldn't take my credit card or my travellers cheques. Consequently, I was forced to use the few American dollars that I had on hand to pay for my fuel.

To my horror, not one store or financial institution in the tiny town of Misaki was willing to accept my Canadian credit card or travellers cheques. I walked and walked through the streets of this tiny, remote fishing village, begging for someone to provide me with some cash or allow usage of my card, but they simply shook their heads as though I was an alien from outer space. I also discovered that not a soul in the town spoke a word of English. I felt like I was captive in a foreign environment with no money, no food, a broken boat and no one who cared.

In desperation, I rummaged through every nook and cranny of *Kluane* to gather whatever food morsels I could find. By this time I had been aboard for 24 hours and was famished. My limited food supplies consisted of flour, sugar, rice, dried milk, several cans of tuna fish, a number of condiments and a few spices. I remember dividing these supplies into tiny piles and rationing out three meals a day for a total of eight days. Breakfast and lunch would essentially be a bannock-style pancakes using flour, sugar and spices. My dinners would include protein, based on canned tuna over a spicy rice concoction. It wasn't my preference but I knew I could manage for eight days, or until I found another solution.

My next task was to fix the head stay and repair the sail; otherwise, I could not leave Misaki. It took all of my strength and agility to lower the head sail, secure it in a sail bag, transfer it into the dinghy and take it to shore. I still remember hoisting it on my back and walking down the dirt road knocking on doors and mimicking the stitching motion in an effort to find someone who could sew the torn sail. Finally, a sweet little old lady ushered me into her living room and agreed to do the repairs. All of my communication was done with hand signals and drawing pictures of whatever I needed. This compassionate woman agreed to have my sail repaired within a week.

It goes without saying that this first week in Misaki was an incredibly depressing and frustrating time. My long days were spent taking vigorous hikes around the deserted bay and into the hinterlands of Japan's rice fields and countryside. I had to avoid any proximity to the few village grocery stores to avoid temptation and longing for food. I eventually called for help on the ham radio and numerous compassionate people from all over the world came to my rescue. Ham operators in Japan sent messages to my family in Canada and I was eventually patched into my husband Michael's phone line to explain my dire situation. Michael agreed to find a solution to my financial crisis and promised to do everything he could to have money transferred to Japan – not knowing how or when.

During my idle time, I continuously cleaned all of the cupboards and interior of *Kluane* knowing that I may need to sell her in Japan. The weather window to cross the North Pacific to Alaska was short and closing quickly. My mind raced between trying to sail her back to Canada or sell her in Japan, so I began to prepare for both eventualities.

On Day 6 of my rationing regime I was packing up some nautical books about the South Pacific that I knew I would no longer need. To my utmost surprise, $600 that had been stashed away for emergencies and totally forgotten about came tumbling out of one book. I could not believe my eyes. It felt like gold. I remember sitting on the settee with two huge handfuls of dollars and throwing it in the air – followed by a feeling of ecstasy as the bills slowly landed on my head, thighs and all around me. I instantly felt like a millionaire. My second round of tears rolled down my cheeks – in this case, they were tears of joy!

"Let the party begin!" I screamed at full volume to the empty walls as I collected all of the bills and then scrambled to quickly get dressed. I jumped into my dinghy with a wad of crisp dollar bills and zoomed at full speed into the dock. My first stop was the marina restaurant where I ordered and devoured a feast of Japanese delights. Still in high gear, I ran into the village and raced through all of the tiny stores grabbing every tasty morsel imaginable - sometimes not even knowing what was inside the package. I bought wine, scotch and cigars! Once my arms were overflowing with bags of food and refreshments, I scurried back to *Kluane* to celebrate this momentous occasion. I never stopped cooking the entire night and after ample wine, scotch and cigars I fell into a deep sleep having experienced one of my best parties ever – by myself and in honour of myself. (Smile.)

During the following few weeks I managed to have the head stay repaired by a local machinist and my newly sewn sail was installed. I took a train to Yokohama and found a yacht broker named Yoshi who was wonderfully engaging and happy to take my listing. By this time I had become very adept at communicating and negotiating using sign language and drawing pictures. Several people made low-ball offers on *Kluane* knowing that I was somewhat desperate to return to Canada, but I was not prepared to accept an outrageously low price.

One dark and stormy night, I was sitting at my navigation station communicating on my ham net with concerned and faithful friends from our South Pacific voyage named Yerger and Margarite Johnston aboard their boat *Asteroid*. Our boats had cruised together from Fiji to Guam over the previous year and *Asteroid* was able to reach me by radio from Thailand. Suddenly, someone was frantically banging on my hull and screaming at me for attention. I ran up the companionway and discovered that Yoshi, my yacht broker, was frantically yelling at me to get off my boat and board his dinghy. The entire scene was puzzling and caught me totally off guard. Why would Yoshi venture an hour away from his home on a stormy night to come to my boat? Why was he in such a panic to get me off my boat?

Yoshi refused to take any time to provide an explanation and continued to holler at me relentlessly. Feeling that I had no choice but to obey, I quickly apprised Yerger of the situation over the ham radio and agreed to report back to him in the morning. We decided that Yerger would call me on the land line at the marina at 10.00am the following morning and I rushed to collect my basic belongings.

Yoshi and I sped at full throttle to the marina dock and he grabbed my hand as we ran to his car in total darkness. Our one-hour car ride to his home in Yokohama was disturbing for me because he could not communicate the reason for the distressful situation that was causing such turmoil. Finally, when we reached his home, he took me to his television. To my dismay, the news was broadcasting news about a huge volcano eruption that was forming an island in the middle of a bay. The eruption was explosive with soaring fire and enormous clouds of smoke billowing from the centre. Yoshi proceeded to draw me a picture of a volcano and a small sailboat alongside the eruption. That sailboat was *Kluane*.

My nervousness was heightened as I listened to the Japanese announcer continuously repeat the word tsunami. I could not interpret whether he was saying that there would be a tsunami or would not be one. The situation became even graver for me when the telephone rang. It was his family calling from Europe. In best our efforts to communicate, I understood that his family had seen the volcano eruption on television in Europe, making me realize that this natural catastrophe made world news. Yoshi's devoted wife eventually ushered me into a Japanese-style bedroom with tatami mats on the floor and indicated that it would be my sleeping area for the night. Soon, the family turned out their lights and I was left alone, lying on my tatami mat to contemplate this extraordinary and frightening situation.

When the house was silent I quietly crept into the living room and located the telephone. I needed to speak to Michael and share this experience. I also needed to hear some comforting words and hear his advice. I tried and tried in desperation to get through to Canada using every tactic imaginable with the operator, but eventually gave up and crawled back to my mat. I tossed and turned for most of the night on the hard woven mat wondering what would become of *Kluane* during the night and what would be my course of action in the morning. Sadly, the novelty of enjoying traditional Japanese hospitality was superseded by my desperate situation and concerns for my boat.

During our traditional early morning breakfast I politely but emphatically asked Yoshi to take me to *Kluane* as soon as possible. I desperately needed to speak with my friend Yerger at our scheduled 10.00am call at the marina. Yoshi complied and hastily drove me to the marina. To my utter disappointment, we were greeted by the marina attendant who advised me that I had just missed a telephone call from Mr Johnston. I will never forget my sunken feeling when I learned of this news. Totally disheartened, I sat on the steps of the Misaki Marina and proceeded to sob. I was unaware that crying in public is offensive in Japanese culture and when I finally lifted my head to look around the entire marina had emptied of people – including the cleaning staff!

Yoshi allowed me some time to collect my thoughts and then took me to *Kluane*. We were in awe at the sight before us as we drove to the boat in his small craft. A new island had, in fact, been born at the end of the bay and *Kluane* was covered with volcanic ash. I thanked Yoshi for his valiant attempt to save me and his extraordinary hospitality during the night. Once he left me to fend for myself in the event of a tsunami, I quickly amassed all of my research aboard to investigate proper procedures for preparation. Collisions with other boats and land-based structures are the biggest hazards in the event of a tsunami, so I ensured that *Kluane* had a lot of surrounding room and hoped for the best. In fact, there was no tsunami and by the end of the day I was ready for my second shot of much-needed scotch!

Yoshi presented me with an acceptable cash offer six weeks after my arrival in Japan with one proviso – that I deliver *Kluane* to Tokyo which was a 48-hour sail from Misaki. I agreed wholeheartedly and asked if he could find me crew for this voyage. Yoshi recommended a capable French sailor named François and plans were set to depart the following Saturday. I provisioned for two people and prepared *Kluane* for our final voyage.

François arrived on schedule along with seven young

Japanese people who spoke no English and had never been aboard a boat. Apparently, they were friends of the purchaser and wanted a ride aboard a sailboat. Shocked, I explained that my food supplies and safety equipment did not provide for seven extra people. They didn't seem to care and I was anxious to set sail, so we immediately untied our lines and were soon bound for Tokyo Harbour. My seven mystery guests were very quiet and sat dutifully in the cabin throughout most of the voyage while François and I took turns at the helm. The fact that François and I were able to communicate in French was a blessing.

The winds were calm for most of the voyage which delayed our arrival into Tokyo Bay by nearly 12 hours. By the time we arrived it was midnight. Making matters worse, Japan's navigation lights are the opposite of the North American navigation system and therefore the green and red channel lights were confusing at first. Four lanes of continual freighter traffic were coming at us from both directions at an average speed of 12 knots so we had to traverse the traffic lanes because of our slower speed. François and I both kept vigilant watch while our guests slept soundly in the cabin.

At approximately 1.00am, one of the guests popped his head into the cockpit and said, "Pamela. Water." Not knowing his reasoning I peered into the dark cabin and saw water sloshing around the cabin floor. I quickly checked the bilges and they were full of water! Water was evident just below the floorboards and it was immediately evident that the cabin was flooding. After clearing the traffic lanes, we stopped the engine and *Kluane* drifted in circles with François on watch. I frantically searched for the apparent leak but could not find the source. The water had a saline taste but I could not distinguish whether or not it was strong enough to be sea water, or just salt grime from the bilge. "Great," I thought. After 35,000 ocean miles, *Kluane* could possibly sink within an hour of her final destination in one of the dirtiest, smelliest harbours in the world!

As a last resort, I scurried around the boat sourcing all of the freshwater lines for any visible or possible leak. To my relief, as I directed my flashlight at the hot water tank, I noticed a continual drip. The hose had fallen off the tank and was pumping fresh water into the boat. I secured the line onto the tank, grabbed every bucket, bowl and pot available and handed each of my sleepy guests a container. "Begin bailing!" I said, as they shook themselves into consciousness. Suddenly, I had an assembly line of dutiful Japanese workers streaming in and out of the boat until the bilges were dry. My anonymous guests had earned their keep!

It took an additional two hours to navigate the long, winding, narrow channel to the marina that *Kluane* would soon call her home. We finally arrived at 4.00am and to my shock and dismay, the future owner was sleeping soundly on the dock with his head resting on a huge duffel bag full of cash – $100,000.00 in total! He was incredibly excited when we pulled into the dock and could not wait to be the proud owner of his new sailboat. I spent the following two hours counting the cash and watched the sun rise without a minute of sleep.

The next two weeks were spent packing and shipping our belongings back to Canada. *Kluane's* new owners were an incredibly hospitable family of renowned Japanese mountain climbers. In fact, one fellow was famous for being part of the Japanese team on their first assent of Everest. Between packing and cleaning they hosted me to a memorable 24-hour kabuki theatre event, as well as numerous evenings of wonderful dining and taking in traditional Japanese highlights.

On my final night aboard *Kluane* I went to sleep confident that her future was in good hands. All of my work was completed. Only one task remained prior to my 6.00am airport pick-up, which was to lower the Canadian flag. I awoke bright and early and made my final cup of coffee. I gathered my strength and forced myself to reach for the lanyard and bring down the flag. Tears began to swell in my eyes. How do you say good-bye to such a cherished treasure that has provided so many meaningful family occasions and memories? The shackle that secured the flag was rusted and I couldn't see how to loosen it through my tears. I tried and tried to undo the clasp but the flag didn't want to let go. Finally, I decided to leave this task to someone else and hoisted the Canadian flag for the very last time. I sat in the cockpit and waited for my ride – with tears of sorrow for the very last time in Japan.

As I disembarked *Kluane*, I tried to find a way to give her a giant hug and kiss. The only remaining artifact of her presence was my treasured log book, which I wrapped securely in my suitcase for the long trip home. Inscribed on the back page was my 'wish-list' that featured a long list of amenities and important characteristics for my next offshore boat. That boat became *Precious Metal* – exactly 10 years later.

APPENDIX II

If Fish Could Talk

Hello, Mr and Mrs Human Being,
Thank you for allowing me to speak to your species today. Before I
begin, I want you to know that on behalf of the millions of marine
creatures in the oceans – we are not pleased with your species. You
should also know the oceans represent 70 percent of this planet.
Every breath you take, every food you eat, every weather system
that you experience, everything in your life – is connected to our
oceans. WE can live without YOU, but YOU cannot live without
US…and time is seriously running out for ALL of us, and the
future of our planet.

ADMIRAL R FUTURE

I AM NOT a scientist, marine biologist, lobbyist, employee or researcher. I am just a simple sailor. A simple sailor who has navigated over 100,000 nautical miles in her lifetime – many single-handed. A sailor who is passionate about the ocean. The ocean is my home.

So why should you pay attention to ME?

Because, cruising sailors see things and places along the world's coastline that most people on our planet don't know exist. We generally sail very slowly and venture into coastal villages and communities that are ignored or bypassed by most people in the world – as tourists, researchers, mega-yachts or freighters. I believe that I ran my last marathon faster that my boat sails, and most of my cruising has been coastal. Most recently along the shores of western Canada, Unites States, South and Central America, and many unique islands along the route, including the Galapagos, Cocos, Las Perlas in Panama and many more.

My love for the oceans and the unique cruising lifestyle began in the early 1980s when my former husband Michael and I had a burning desire to sail around the world. Our children, Sam and Charlie were ages 10 and 4 respectively, and after taking numerous courses and extensive preparation we set sail from British Columbia, Canada, on a two-and-a-half year voyage that would change my life forever. Our 35,000-nautical-mile voyage took us through the exquisite islands of the South Pacific Ocean to New Zealand and north to Japan – at a time when there was no GPS; sails and a sextant were our only navigation tools.

I fell in love during this voyage. I fell in love with stunning sunrises and sunsets. I fell in love with snorkelling through brilliantly coloured coral reefs with an abundance of fascinating tropical fish. I fell in love with having the ability to catch our daily sustenance and exist primarily off the land and sea. I fell in love with sailing past pristine tropical islands surrounded by clear turquoise oceans with depths as far as the eye could see. I fell in love with the cruising lifestyle, where one can take one's family and small home anywhere in the world that's by the ocean and live in these remote communities; eat their food and enjoy their customs and culture.

Upon our return to Canada in 1989, I vowed that we would raise our children wholeheartedly and enjoy a traditional lifestyle; however, we would also strive to earn enough money to once again return to cruising on the ocean. The sea beckoned, and I could never let go.

Fast forward 30 years. Sam and Charlie became terrific young adults and married to wonderful daughters-in-law. I rode an outstanding wave in my career in the investment business in the 1990s and retired in 2001. Sadly, I was no longer married; however, in my divorce settlement I was able to hang on to one bright glimmer of hope that represented a positive future: I got the boat!

Precious Metal is a luxurious steel 47-foot custom-design cutter rig built in 1999 to sail anywhere in the world. She could have been called 'Wish List' because I had written a wish list in the back of my log book from the South Pacific voyage that included all of her exclusive amenities: bathtub, wash and dryer, walk-in engine room with a full-size work bench, cherrywood interior, and the best sails and rigging that money could buy.

In spite of my divorce, and my 50th year being the darkest of my life, I was determined to follow my dream of sailing off into the sunset and return to the cruising lifestyle that I once loved so intoxicatingly. In 2008, accompanied by my little dog Riley, we set sail on a five-year, 25,000 ocean adventure of a lifetime: down the west coast of United States, Mexico, South and Central America, Panama and Galapagos.

Tragically, this time was different. Almost every harbour that *Precious Metal* anchored in was filthy. Disgustingly filthy with garbage, dirty water and sewer smells. Beaches along every coastline were smothered with garbage – mostly plastics. My water-maker filters were clogged with horrible gunk and needed replacing regularly – as opposed to the six months stated in the instructions. If I found a coral reef, most of the coral was broken or bleached and tropical fish were rare. Jelly fish – which are the cockroaches of the oceans – were so prevalent that I went weeks at a time surrounded by insidious blooms. Much of the ocean water contained red tide or was bright green filled with an over-abundance of algae. Local fishermen would go further and further into the ocean to catch fewer and fewer fish and return each day with a pathetically tiny catch to feed their families.

Two years into my voyage I arrived into Lima, Peru, and decided to investigate my observations. During my seven months in Lima I devoted considerable time towards research and writing to the best and brightest in the marine research field throughout the world in an attempt to analyse the severity of our ocean crisis. Those agencies that did reply had similar responses: "The ocean situation is serious, and a lot worse than you think."

Further research has indicated that there are countless agencies throughout the world that are all deeply concerned – many with a doomsday scenario, and many still marginally hopeful. Clearly, everyone in the know – the best and brightest in marine research and science – all agree that our oceans and planet are in serious danger. In 2009, one of my many heroes in marine research, TED prize-winner Sylvia Earle, gave humans 10 years in her acceptance speech – 10 years to make a difference for the thousands of years on this planet and the future of our children and future generations. That was five years ago.

Since then, our Great Pacific Garbage Patch has gained a deplorable reputation for hosting millions of pounds of garbage – some reports admit that it's the size of the continent of the United States. Midway Island, the closest land to our biggest garbage vortex in the Pacific, is a graveyard for albatrosses and marine life – all filled with plastics in their guts. Massive commercial fishing fleets with nets up to 50 miles long continue to sweep the ocean floor to the extent that 90 percent of our big important predator fish (sharks and tuna) are now gone from the oceans, and at this rate of mismanagement there will be no more fish on this planet in 2050. Fifty percent of our coral reefs are dead – which host over 25 percent of fish in the oceans. Ocean acidity and surface temperatures are becoming irreversibly imbalanced causing climate change, rising sea levels and forced relocation of many marine habitat. Over 405 oxygen-free dead zones have been located in coastal ocean regions – the largest is 77,000 square miles in the Gulf of Mexico. Why are humans allowing this to happen with no apparent major outcry?

I say to myself: "Kate Middleton wears a new hat, and it becomes headline news around the world. A movie star gets a DUI, or a politician gets busted in a sex scandal and the world is all over the story. Yet the heart and lungs of our every planet are in imminent danger and no one really seems to pay much attention."

Last year (2013) the United States spent $680 billion on defence, and the world spent $1.7 trillion. If they don't address the survival of our planet there won't be anything to defend. Making matters worse are the developing countries of Brazil, Russia, India and China who represent of half of the world's population, entering a new era of developing from poverty to middle-class lifestyles with no education, infra-structure or wherewithal of addressing sustainable environmental standards – in the air or the oceans. There are no international borders when it comes to garbage or air emissions. These are global issues requiring global solutions. Why isn't the world taking a stand?

Are the oceans 'out of sight, out of mind'? Are humans too distracted with their daily lives or care about the survival of our planet? Will it take too much human sacrifice to change our behaviour so it's best just to ignore our reality? Or – is it because fish can't talk? Fish can't Tweet. They are not LinkedIn. They can't represent themselves and cry out for attention.

My recent speaking presentation at the Toronto International Boat Show included a small segment by a special guest, Admiral R Future. The highly respected 'Admiral' expounded with tremendous passion about the human disregard for his oceans by highlighting details about garbage, over-fishing, acidity, surface temperature change, coral reef extinction and dead zones. The Admiral's presentation was enthusiastically applauded by a well-meaning audience of converted sympathizers who solemnly sat in the theatre overwhelmed by a deep sense of helplessness.

"What can we do about it?" asked one despondent woman in the audience. Naturally, I've had a lot of time to think about our ocean crisis. The solutions are complex and will require tremendous sacrifices by humans. We need to change the way we think and behave, and I'm not sure whether we're willing to take on this challenge – despite the extreme consequences to our planet. I believe that it will take a major disaster to heighten human attention.

Environmental education should be mandatory at all levels in schools around the globe. Media and politicians need to make environmental sustainability, and oceans in particular, their top priority. We should be waking up each day with front page news about regions of the world that are becoming protected (only 0.8 of one percent of our oceans are protected), new ways to sustain our planet, research and development of new technologies that will help resolve our ocean crisis.

My philosophical challenge is that this all essentially

happened in the last 30 years on OUR watch – when the hippies from the 1970s became yuppies. Equally perplexing is that I honestly can't think of who will have enough influence to alter the minds of our politicians and corporate stakeholders. Other than Warren Buffet, who still lives in his modest home in Omaha, Nebraska, most of the influential people in the world are also the biggest culprits with gargantuan mansions, lavish 'shop 'til they drop' lifestyles and 100-foot mega yachts. How can they possibly effect change?

Who will lead this incredibly important revolutionary turn towards a sustainable ocean and planet? Perhaps Kate Middleton? I know that I will do everything in my power to raise human awareness and influence those around me…

Although I'm just a simple sailor…

APPENDIX III

Introductory Step-by-Step Guide to Boat Maintenance

For Women from a Woman's Perspective

OW! SO YOU'RE interested in embracing the ever-challenging, often frustrating and incredibly satisfying world of boat maintenance! Terrific. The title of my book is fitting, because rarely a day goes by without a tiny voice from within whispering, "Pamela, what were you thinking?" Unquestionably, the greatest number of 'what was I thinking' moments have related to the maintenance (and repairs) of my 50,000-pound beast *Precious Metal* in distant, remote, often solo, offshore situations.

Truthfully, when I departed Canada I thought I was pretty competent with the workings of my boat. I didn't know what I didn't know. Certainly, I knew how to change my filters, alternator belts, oil and simple tasks; but I had no comprehension of the magnitude of work that's required to maintain every system on my boat. Mostly, because I always hired people, or relied on my male partner to take on that role. Due to persistence as well as necessity, I'm now pretty confident with most of the systems aboard my boat. That said, I'm also fully aware that many surprises are still in store!

I hate to stereotype; however, few woman are raised and socialized in the field of mechanics, tools, electronics, filter systems, battery systems and so on. Few women, including most of the offshore female sailors that I've met, make a valiant attempt to understand the 'real' workings of a boat. The actual sailing and navigation of my boat is incidental in comparison to what I refer to as the 'blue' jobs (versus the 'pink' tasks that are traditionally female). As a single-hander I've had to master both. Furthermore, partners on a boat inadvertently take on roles which become routine and unquestionably accepted. How often would you hear the husband say to his wife, "Okay honey, I'll go down and make the sandwiches while you replace the wiring on the bilge pump."

One has to be prepared to get dirty and spend time in precarious positions aboard the boat that simply aren't lady-like. That said, it's incredibly gratifying to take apart a mechanical or electrical boat system, maintain or repair it and successfully assemble it all back together. Furthermore, boat systems are generally quite simple and make a lot of sense. Although initially daunting and definitely filthy, boat maintenance can be learned by anyone.

Aside from the gratification that comes with conquering the art of successfully completing a maintenance project, there are a number of really good reasons why every boater should be competent in boat maintenance and repairs. The reality of boats is that if a part or system hasn't been maintained properly, it will break down and will need to be repaired. Furthermore, if you haven't maintained it, you won't likely know how to repair it; nor will you likely have the spare parts and available tools. You can do maintenance at your leisure; however, a repair is most often required at an inopportune time, under duress and possibly in a dangerous situation. Finally, knowledge is power. The more you understand your boat, the more independent you become, which ultimately results in a higher level of fulfilment and enjoyment.

As I type this document in *Precious Metal's* raised salon during a wonderful sail from Nicaragua to El Salvador, I look around my boat wondering where to begin on the topic of maintenance. Every boat is different and has different systems to maintain. Some people have unlimited budgets, while others need to be frugal. Furthermore, each person's background knowledge, physical fitness and skill level is different. I mention physical fitness because at times my boat maintenance and repair projects are incredibly demanding physically. I refer to my boat as my gymnasium and often have to use creative levers and pulleys in order compensate for what most men would find easy – and I've always been known to be athletic.

Let's get started.

Find your grubbiest clothes, eye glasses if needed, some rags, medical (latex or vinyl) examination gloves and a good sense of humour – as you'll need all of the above! By the way, I've never met a mechanic who had nice fingernails. If you care about your nails, invest in some snug-fitting medical gloves. They can't be loose or they'll get caught up in everything and cause you frustration. Another trick to protect your nails from getting stained with grease and grime is to scratch your nails along a bar of soap before you begin working. This will fill in the gap between your fingers and nails with soap. Just be sure to have a good nail brush when you're finished or your next scrumptious meal will be garnished with some horribly tasting chunks of soap!

As a fun side-note, if you're wondering what to do with your old nail polish, I use it to paint the measurements on my anchor chain. There's usually a variety of colours hanging around and nail polish seems to last much longer than traditional paint. I've now run out of old nail polish and use coloured, plastic cable/zip straps, but the nail polish added a fun touch and my male sailing companions were quite amused and envious!

The following are some introductory steps to follow that explain how to learn about your boat, its operating systems and essential maintenance protocol:

1. Design a spreadsheet
This should cover all of the following:
- engine maintenance
- fuel system maintenance:
- filter systems

- alternators and belts,
- batteries
- cables
- oil changes
- pumps for every working part
- electrical connectors throughout the boat
- bilge cleaning
- rust work (rust never sleeps!)
- wood maintenance
- deck work
- canvass work
- rigging maintenance
- sail maintenance
- dinghy and outboard maintenance
- water-maker maintenance
- gas generator maintenance
- hose clamps throughout the entire boat
- mould cleaning and prevention
- stanchions and lifelines
- safety equipment
- anchor chain
- boat bottom
- sheets and lines
- head maintenance
- general cleaning and polishing

2. Find Yourself a Coach

An experienced, patient, good natured, understanding person who is savvy with boats. I need to warn you, finding the right person may be your biggest challenge! If you have a partner, it would be fun to work through this process together. Don't try to be a hero. I still ask for guidance when I'm attempting something for the first time – even if I have to call from my satellite phone. There are so many subtle tricks of the trade that aren't written in the books and manuals. It can be dangerous if you're unaware of the chemicals, toxins and electrical forces that you're exposed to in certain projects. Also, a novice could easily cause a lot of damage. A knowledgeable person will not only ensure that the job is done properly the first time, but also, they will know the proper tools to use and their applications. Boats are different from cars and houses insofar as they require stainless steel products or parts that are not subject to the corrosive effects of saltwater. They also have to withstand tremendous static and dynamic forces and work flawlessly under severe adverse weather conditions. Also, keep in mind there's generally less accessibility to boat parts and systems.

3. Identify all of the systems on your boat

Take the list of maintenance projects that I highlighted above in my maintenance regime paragraph and identify on your boat all of the systems that are mentioned. It may be a bit of a treasure hunt because boat systems are usually tucked away in some unassuming, cramped place. If you're unsure, ask your coach if you have these systems aboard your boat and where they are located. Find out whether you have diagrams of your electrical, mechanical and various boat systems. Every part and system will (or should) have a manual with a maintenance program and detailed description in the back section. You can download most manuals on your computer in order to save paper and/or as a backup. A number of books have been written on boat maintenance; however, I find them frustrating because they're not specific to my boat. Individual specific manuals are preferable. Also, depending on the sophistication of your boat, labelling the various hoses, wiring, sea cocks, etc will be advantageous. If you have a label printer, use strong invisible tape to secure the labels.

4. Learn to do everything yourself

Be sure to tell your coach that you want to learn to do everything yourself. Often helpful people will show me how to do it, but I never actually learn the technique unless I do it myself. Also, I find that despite their wonderful intentions, experienced (men) people tend to think I'm as strong as they are and as savvy about how to use the various tools. Then they leave, having tightened the part so tight that I can't undo it when I need to. They also make the assumption that I've been using these tools – which are second nature to them – throughout my entire life. This is about *you* learning and not about *them* showing off their knowledge or prowess. As we know, women learn differently from men.

5. The right tools
You have your manuals and diagrams. Now you need your tools. Having the right tool and knowing how to use it was a big eye-opener for me. I know it sounds naive, but my original knowledge of tools was pretty basic. The world of tools is massive. Not only the kinds of tools, but sizes and functions. I now colour-code my tools with tape for each project so that I don't have to try and re-try until I get the right type or size. Keep in mind that tools, as well as screws and bolts etc, come in metric and universal sizes, so you'll need to become adept with your fractions. We all know about 1/4-inch, 1/2-inch and 3/4-inch measurements – but these get divided into 8ths and 16ths millimetres and all sorts of combinations that I still have to resurrect from my early childhood education. I try to purchase my tools in automotive stores and general hardware stores when they're not boat-specific. Any products labelled with the word 'marine' will be marked up substantially.

In your tool supply you should have (and know how to use): a good socket set, drill – with a complete set of strong drill bits, wrench set, needle-nose and regular pliers, screwdrivers in several sizes with different heads (Phillips, Robertson and straight), wire cutters, a skill saw with sharp blades, (what I call) 'upside-down screwdrivers' which are mostly used for hose clamps (I believe they're called socket drivers but I've re-named them because I'm usually upside-down when I use them...), a good hammer, vice-grips and crescent wrench(es) – several sizes. This should start you off with a basic supply of necessary tools and as time and comfort develops, so will your tool supplies.

With each project, you'll need a variety of sized screws, bolts and hose clamps– all specific to the systems, hoses and fittings of your boat. If you don't know about hose clamps, ask your coach as they're really important and need to be stainless steel. Take a magnet to the store when you're buying them; stainless steel, unlike iron or other types of steel, is not magnetic and so won't be picked up by a magnet. If you can pick up a clamp (or any other metal object that should be stainless steel), you don't want it on your boat! Note that stainless steel comes in a variety of grades, so be sure you get good quality.

Depending on the part that you're maintaining, you'll possibly need a new filter, new hose, gasket, impeller, etc. Always have a spare of every part or system aboard the boat and keep a running inventory list.

6. Cleaners and lubricants
Next you need to acquire and learn about cleaners and lubricants, Teflon tape, water resistant grease, cable/zip ties, sealants, cleaners and a (hand) cleaning solvent. When you take something apart you'll be needing some or all of the above – depending on the part or system – to put it back together.

7. Start a maintenance book
Keep a digital camera aboard and start your own maintenance book. As you take each system or part apart, take a photo of each stage and file the photos onto your computer – along with your downloaded maintenance manuals. This will save you a lot of grief when you're putting it back together and of course, when you have to maintain it in the future. I once took my entire stove apart to change the burners and after reassembling the entire unit, with dozens of screws, there was one screw left over! (Sigh.) I had to take the entire stove apart and reassemble it to find the home of the one extra screw.

Also, draw your own diagrams that you will understand. Use whatever terminology makes sense to you because it probably won't be professional, but at least it will make sense to you. Using your manual references, draw up a spreadsheet of how often each system or part needs to be addressed and leave a space to record the date for each time you repair or maintain it.

8. Start simple

I suggest that you begin with a simple system: learn it well so that you fully understand the entire process of the operation. Once you're comfortable with that system and have recorded it properly, know the tools, labelled the tools, inventoried the spare parts, etc, then you can progress to the next part or system. Trying to take the entire boat on all at once will become confusing and frustrating and intimidating.

Let's start with hose clamps. It's a simple task and will ensure that you find your way throughout many of the 'blue' systems aboard your boat. Every hose leading from your water system, engine system, head system, bilge system (and more) requires hose clamps (I usually use two) to attach the hose to whatever fitting or part that it is connected to. A broken hose clamp on certain parts of your boat (drive shaft, exhaust, etc) can be a show-stopper if you don't have a spare. Take your (probably yellow) upside-down screw driver and find all of your hose clamps. Check to see if they're rusted and need replacing. Check to see if they're tight. Make sure that the tightening bolt is facing towards you for easy access. I think you'll be surprised at how many hose clamps are on your boat. Take note of all the sizes and be sure you have lots of spares (of all sizes) in your inventory. Mark the date in your maintenance log. I usually have 'Hose Clamp Day' every six months, or as necessary.

9. Learn the fuel system

Next, I suggest that you learn the fuel system. It's a system that is critical in terms of running any motorized boat and it's easy to learn. Most boats run on diesel, but not all. It will introduce you into the world of smelly 'Eau de Diesel' and will likely infiltrate your hands and clothes. You should follow the fuel line hoses and learn the flow of diesel (or gas) from the fuel tank(s) to the engine and fuel return line back to the tank. How do you access your tanks if you had to check inside? You should become proficient at changing all of the filters throughout the system and bleeding the system. There's a handy and inexpensive harness that some boats have – what one might call an 'internal fuel polishing system'. It's also important to understand your boat's mileage and fuel consumption. What factors will change this consumption (currents, seas, winds, dirty bottom)? How often do the filters need to be changed? Dirty fuel is a common problem on a boat – particularly in more remote places. Learn the causes of dirty fuel. Be sure you have a good filter when you fill the boat and use fuel additives to prevent algae and foreign growth in the fuel tanks. Most experts recommend that fuel tanks should always be filled whenever possible to prevent condensation. I installed a vacuum gauge on my filter that shows when I have an air leak, as well as a water alarm that detects water in my fuel. I strongly recommend having both.

10. Filters

Once you've mastered changing your fuel filters, all of the other filters should be easy. Find them and change each one – documenting your diagrams, tools and notes as well as inventory the necessary spare parts. Changing the oil filter can be messy. My trick is to wrap the entire filter in a zip-lock baggie as I unscrew the filter. Excess oil gets collected in the baggie as well as the filter and then I simply zip the whole thing up and take it to the nearest oil dispensing location. With experience you shouldn't spill a drop!

11. Understand your electrical system

Next should be a certain level of competency in your knowledge regarding your electrical systems. Mastering the simple concepts of AC (alternating) and DC (direct) currents are essential. Just remember that anything you use that has a plug requires AC power and is usually 110 or 220 volts. DC currents run off your house battery system. An inverter is the piece of equipment that converts your DC to AC. When you're plugged into shore power (using a plug outlet) you're using AC power. One loose, corroded or shorted wire in any of your boat systems and electronics (including navigation) can and will shut it down. Don't expect to become a full-fledged electrician instantly, but you should learn how to check fuses, wiring connections and if necessary splice a new connector to replace a broken or shorted wire. Your new electrical kit should include the following: a splicing tool that measures and cuts all the different sizes of wires and casings, a wide assortment of connectors (male and female) and a voltage meter. You will also need heat/shrink wrap (essentially a rubber-looking hose that slips over the new connection that you heat with a lighter flame and it shrinks over your new connection to secure it together), fuses – both regular glass ones and in-line ones, and wiring of various sizes. Again, once you become confident and proficient with your electrical expertise your kit will expand to include more items.

I'm deferring further reference to electrical systems to an expert so that you can do it hands on with supervision during the initial stages. This person should work with you to trace all of your wiring aboard and then teach you the basics of wiring. Once you discover how easy it is you'll be changing lights, installing new equipment and expanding to three-way switches that are often used on a boat (red, white and off).

Also, whenever possible switch your lighting to LED. It's cost-effective and helps to preserve our precious planet. Remember that when you install a new piece of electronic equipment or anything that involves power, you should remove the electrical diagrams of your old system or part and replace it with the new one(s). Remove all of those former manuals at the same time from your inventory and maintenance book.

12. Time to address the bilge

If you've made it this far, it's time to address the bilge; which, for me is the yuckiest job and warrants the grubbiest clothes, gloves and a really good attitude. The bilge in your boat is where all of the liquids and crud ends up and it needs to be pumped out via your bilge pump. If you don't maintain the bilge on a regular basis, the pump will get blocked, or the switch that activates the pump will malfunction – either due to blockage or wiring corrosion. It's really important to keep the bilge area clean because if the pump doesn't work, your boat won't be able to eject water and other fluids (often oil and diesel) that collect in the bilge and the boat could eventually sink! Your bilge will be found at the lowest point of the boat and often it has a designated well. This usually makes it difficult to access.

There are bilge cleaners in marine stores which I used to pour into my bilge when the boat was in rolling seas. The bilge cleaner will theoretically break down the crud. I now use a combination of dish soap, water and vinegar instead, because it's a lot cheaper and easier to find. Remember, anything that has the word 'marine' on the label is usually double in price. Cleaners will help keep the pump unclogged, but it's still important to clean around the pump and switch on a regular basis just to be on the safe side. Some pumps clip into a stand and others are attached in a variety of ways. You need to lift it out and clean the bottom so that water can flow freely into the pump. The float switch that activates the automatic pump should be close by and wired into the pump. Make sure it's free to move up and down and sitting in a clean environment.

13. The battery system, motor and ground tackle

The battery system and motor are your next priorities, not necessarily in that order. If you plan to anchor frequently, then your ground tackle (anchor and chain) should also be high on your list of maintenance priorities. I strongly recommend that you address each of these topics seriously and with a competent, certified person at your side. Again, what you learn in a course, or in a book will give you good basic knowledge; however, it probably won't apply specifically to your boat. It took me hours of endless frustration to learn to use the available resources and expertise of other people.

Once all of these important systems are mastered, you'll have found your way around most of the critical aspects of your boat and the rest of the list will fall into place.

As you can imagine, I have only scratched the surface of boat maintenance protocol. I believe if you follow the recommendations outlined above you'll have enough information to get started and you'll be well on your way towards properly maintaining your boat. Most notably, if you've accomplished any or all of the above, you should be feeling very proud.

About the Author

Toronto-born Pamela Roy Bendall was raised in Montreal, Quebec, and has lived in Vancouver, Victoria, Port Hardy and most recently the Pacific Ocean. Prior to her decision to sail off into the sunset, she had established an impressive professional, intellectual and athletic profile. With a Masters Degree in Communication (Royal Roads University, Victoria), she has worked as a Realtor, Investment Advisor, radio columnist for CBC and was a national level gymnast in

her youth. She has completed four marathons, navigated the Marblehead Ocean Race from Boston to Halifax, the Victoria to Maui Yacht Race and has sailed over 100,000 miles. Her love for adventure travel has taken her to over 100 countries in the world including many majestic mountain ranges in Bhutan, Nepal and Peru. In 1996, she obtained the honour of being the first female in Canada to win the Investment Dealer's Association of Canada Award of Distinction.

Her first book, entitled *Kids for Sail* (Orca Book Publishers), is about her two-year ocean sail from Canada to New Zealand and Japan with her former husband and two young children and was published in 1990. When she's not sailing, Pamela enjoys being a mother to her two adult sons Sam and Charlie, two daughters-in-law Lizz and Catherine and the grandmother to her two precious grandchildren, Maddy and George.

Visit Pamela's website
www.pamelabendall.com